THE MANCHESTER MARTYRS

WILLIAM PHILIP ALLEN

MICHAEL LARKIN

MICHAEL O'BRIEN (GOULD)

THE MANCHESTER MARTYRS

the story of a Fenian Tragedy

PAUL ROSE

LAWRENCE & WISHART
1970

SBN 85315 209 8

Made and Printed in Britain by
The Camelot Press Ltd., London and Southampton

Acknowledgements

To Tom Redmond and Jimmy McGill whose pamphlet published in 1963 stimulated a profound interest in what was until then a shadowy episode in the history of Manchester and Ireland and in particular to Tom who gave generous help in tracing books and pamphlets.

To the staff of the National Library, Dublin, the Local History section of the Manchester Central Library, the British Museum newspaper section at Colindale and the House of Commons Library. To Dr. Menhennet of the Research Division of the House of Commons Library. To Miss Joan Vermuelen and Mr. Richard Lee who assisted in research into contemporary journals.

To Kevin Macnamara, M.P., for reading the first draft manuscript and Michael McGuire, M.P., for his interest and advice. To Mr. Fitzmorris, Mrs. Kelly and Mr. T. C. O'Hara of the Manchester Martyrs Commemoration Committee which has preserved the memory of the Manchester Martyrs in the city where they were executed. To Mrs. Diana Baty for information on Colonel Kelly. To Paddy Byrne of the Campaign for Democracy in Ulster and to Mrs. Adele O'Shaughnessy for typing the first draft manuscript.

To my dedicated secretary, Mrs. Sharon Genasci and to the Auditor of Trinity College, Dublin, Mr. Ashe, who introduced me to one of the most recent contributions to the literature of Fenianism.

To all those descendants of the Irish Immigrants of a century ago whose recollections added colour, substance and human interest to the documents, books, journals and newspapers which form the story of the Manchester Martyrs and their times. And finally to Mr. Seamus O'Kelly whose compact publication *The Bold Fenian Men* is one of the few contemporary histories which understands the social implications of Fenianism and its place in the historical continuity that led from 1798 to 1916.

Contents

"To come to the help of Ireland is equally to come to the help of England."

VICTOR HUGO

Introduction

The turbulent and bloody history of Anglo-Irish relations reached a high-water mark in 1798 and 1916 with the risings of the United Irishmen and with the Easter rebellion which was to lead to an Ireland free and sovereign but unhappily divided. Names like Theobold Wolfe Tone, Robert Emmet, Daniel O'Connell, Charles Stewart Parnell, Michael Davitt, Padraic Pearse and James Connolly flash across the pages of Irish history like meteorites. Their deeds are legendary, and few nations have produced so many heroes and martyrs whose peculiar talent lay in combining a romantic lyricism with direct and frequently violent action in the cause of national freedom.

The highest expression of their objects was the vision of Theobold Wolfe Tone:

> To subvert the tyranny of our execrable Government; to break the connection with England, the never-failing source of all our political evils; and to assert the independence of my country—these were my objects. To unite the whole people of Ireland, to abolish the memory of past dissensions, and to substitute the common name of Irishman in place of the denominations of Protestant, Catholic and Dissenter—these were my means.

For his part in the rising of '98 Wolfe Tone was sentenced to be hanged after fighting with great courage; but rather than allow himself to be hanged, in a last act of defiance he took his own life the night before his impending execution. Robert Emmett was to be hanged, drawn and quartered only five years later, after a last desperate effort to break free from the chains which bound the Irish to England and to its system of landlordism in Ireland. Those chains had been welded more firmly when the Act of Union bound the Parliaments of England and Ireland together from the first day of January, 1801.

It was to take more than a century before the fetters were broken.

Everything from Constitutional Parliamentary opposition to agrarian demonstrations was used by the Irish as weapons. There was no Gandhi to lead Ireland to independence through a creed of non-violence, and the saddest aspect of those years was that ultimately it was the method of violence which was to lead to an Irish Free State.

Bracketed between 1798 and 1916 is one year which stands out as the link in this chain of events and which saw the peak of the movement which continued the traditions of the past and ultimately provided the inspiration for the men who were to take Ireland through a traumatic fight for freedom and an equally tragic civil war. That year was 1867, and the movement was Fenianism, or the Irish Republican Brotherhood. One of its most dramatic exploits was to take place in an English provincial city in the heart of what was the cradle of the English industrial revolution.

On the night of Friday, 22nd November, 1867, a strange sight would have greeted the casual passer-by at Salford Gaol, Manchester. About 30 feet above the ground a part of the prison wall had been removed to provide a platform with access from behind. Upon this platform, barely visible through the gloom, was the ghastly shape of the cross-beamed gallows hung round with black drapery. This was the stage upon which was to be enacted the gruesome spectacle that was to be the culmination of one of the most daring feats of the Irish patriots, the rescue of two Fenian leaders, Colonel Kelly and Captain Deasy.

In its own way this exploit and the subsequent execution of three Irishmen in England has the same significance for the nineteenth century that the 1916 uprising and its aftermath had for the twentieth. Its impact upon Irish—and English—opinion is incalculable. One result was that "the executions aroused in the mind of one, who had been hitherto politically immature and indifferent, a first consciousness of the Irish problem. He was hotly indignant about the fate of the 'Manchester Martyrs'. It was his first identification with the Irish nation and the beginning of the political awakening of Charles Stewart Parnell."[1]

The scene outside the prison must have aroused the disgust of anyone with the sensitive disposition of a Parnell. The crowd was dense, well supplied by the gin palaces of Deansgate and the portable beer and coffee stalls. The crowd laughed, sang, smoked, scuffled, drank and fought. These brutalised victims of an urban environment the squalor

[1] J. Abels, *The Parnell Tragedy.*

of which beggars description had no sympathy for or understanding of the Fenian cause. There was no pity for the three men who were spending their last hours within those immense and impenetrable prison walls, only a sense of expectation of the thrill and horror to be afforded by the execution a few hours later.

But there were others in England who understood and sympathised with the aspirations of the condemned men and their movement, if not always with their methods. And if it achieves nothing more, this narrative seeks to show the bond of sympathy which has united many Englishmen with the cause of national independence in Ireland. This bond of sympathy is easily overlooked in many Irish histories, and could easily be forgotten in reading such an eye-witness account of that scene as was set down by Father Gadd, the Roman Catholic priest who stayed with the men and comforted them to the last:

> A crowd of inhuman ghouls from the purlieus of Deansgate and the slums of the City and the Borough had been gathered for hours in the streets abutting on the gaol and had made the night and early morning hideous with the raucous bacchanalian strains of "Champagne Charlie", "John Brown" and "Rule, Britannia". No Irish mingled with the throng to gaze on the scene on the scaffold. They had obeyed the instructions of their Clergy. Throughout Manchester and Salford, silent congregations with tear-stained faces and hearts throbbing with a thousand emotions assembled in the various churches for a celebration of early Mass for the eternal welfare of the young Irishmen doomed to die a dreadful death that morning.[1]

Indeed, this was to be no ordinary execution. The whole might of authority seemed to be determined that the extreme penalty should be exacted. By morning, the whole area from which any view of the spectacle might be obtained was protected by strong barricades, six or eight on the Manchester side alone. The civil authorities, acting on the instructions of the Home Office, had taken possession of New Bailey Street the day before and under the command of a Captain Sylvester it was policed by 500 men drawn from the Manchester, Salford and County forces. The Manchester side of the river, Stanley Street, Albert Bridge and a short distance along New Bailey Street, was occupied by the Manchester police force under Captain Palin.

[1] Recalled in O'Dea's book, *Story of the Old Faith in Manchester.*

Five hundred soldiers in and around the prison were augmented by 2,000 ordinary and special constables occupying the surrounds of the prison and the area between the spectators. The motley band of specials, distinguished from the crowd only by their white sleeve badges and short truncheons, performed their duties with gusto.

But this was not all: a large detachment of troops from the 72nd Highlanders was on duty at the prison and a squadron of the Eighth Hussars was stationed at the front in Stanley Street with another battery in reserve within the prison walls. During the night a strong body of infantry had occupied the railway viaduct overlooking the north side of the prison. This was the only point from which the specially constructed scaffold might reasonably be attacked. Salford railway station was occupied by the reserves of that force and all the traffic in or out was stopped. "In short, between midnight and six o'clock this morning, a walk through the streets produced the impression that the city was in a state of siege."[1]

Here, in the cradle of an Industrial Revolution which made possible Britain's sway over five continents, no precaution was too great against those whose daring might lead them to attempt yet another rescue to release the three Irishmen in the condemned cell.

There seemed little that was remarkable about those three men other than their courage; only one of them possessed military experience. But the Fenian Movement of which they were part was feared by the English authorities. Named after the heroic militia led by Finn Mac Cumhall which defended Ireland in the saga of Ossian (Oisin-Gaelic), the Fenian Movement, otherwise known as the Irish Republican Brotherhood, had spread widely as a secret revolutionary society which aimed at securing Ireland's political freedom by exploiting every opportunity to injure Britain's interests. In 1914 another variation of the name was to be adopted by Padraic Pearse, who, in his historic address to the boys of Ireland said: "We bear a very noble name and inherit very noble traditions, for we are called after the Fianna of Fionn, that legendary companionship which, according to legend, flourished in Ireland in the second and third centuries of the Christian Era." Thus the Fenians gave way to the Fianna, their logical successors, an indication of the uniquely Irish character of the movement.

Fenianism became a more serious menace to English rule in Ireland when it was reinforced by many Irish Americans who had served on both sides during the American Civil War, gaining an insight into and

[1] *Annual Register*, 1867.

experience of combat which they were to carry with them across the Atlantic back to the land from whence they or their fathers had come.

Forced from their smallholdings and faced with the choice of starvation or emigration, Irishmen were producing a new urban stratum of the working class in Britain and the United States. Some had acquired money, rank and influence in the States and formed a reserve of financial and moral support for the Irish cause. As the "Soldiers Song" was to acknowledge—"Some have come from the land across the wave". It was this element which was to provide the backbone and much of the leadership for the Fenian sympathisers both in Ireland and in areas with large Irish populations such as Manchester.

"To give an accurate estimate of the number of Fenians and Fenian sympathisers in Manchester and within a circuit of fifty miles of it was utterly impossible, but I have heard them put down at upwards of 50,000,"[1] wrote one contemporary commentator, although this suggests a broader definition of Fenians that would seem acceptable in retrospect.

It is not the purpose of this account to describe the indignities and suffering which had been the lot of so many Irishmen and Irishwomen in the years before, nor the struggles of English workers for elementary rights during the same period. Suffice it to say that the great potato famine and the coffin ships which carried their wretched human cargo away from their native land had created a mood of despair in which only the creation of secret societies (in keeping with the agrarian societies that answered terror by landlords with similar acts of terror during the previous century) bent upon armed resistance appeared to be the answer to Ireland's problems. In this mood, national sentiment frequently sublimated the economic woes which were the lot of vast numbers of Irish people.

Since the devastation and depopulation of Judaea at the hands of the Roman Empire, no nation had been dispersed and depopulated as had Ireland, which today supports only half the population, North and South, that it had in 1840. Indeed, between 1841 and 1866 the population of Ireland fell to little more than half in a period of only twenty-five years. Thus, the Fenian movement was bred out of poverty, famine and despair; but above all it was a national protest against the trampling on national pride which many Irishmen, from the men of '98 onwards, had fought with a recklessness typified by the very exploit

[1] C. G. Smith, *The Manchester Outrage*.

for which these three men were to give up their lives on that cold and foggy November morning.

Their names, Allen, Larkin and O'Brien, are now legend. Their monument stands in St. Joseph's Cemetery, Moston, Manchester, the author's own constituency. But what sort of men were they? Were they guilty of murder? What was the Fenian Movement which inspired them? What really happened in the streets of Manchester just over a century ago? Anthony Glynn in his book *High upon the Gallows Tree* has drawn many of the threads together, but it is remarkable that no attempt has been made to analyse this event and assess its historical significance.

Above all it is a matter of some importance today to throw light, not only upon the rescue, trial and execution which make up the personal drama of the Manchester Martyrs, but to know something of the relationship of the Fenians with radical, socialist and labour movements in England in this period—a topic which merits a thorough historical study of its own.

For much of the story relating to the rescue, apart from trial witnesses and contemporary newspapers, one must inevitably rely heavily upon a historic account published forty years later on 4th January, 1908, by one of the principal actors in the drama, Edward O'Meaghar Condon. It was only his American citizenship that saved him from the gallows. O'Leary's, Denvir's and Devoy's recollections throw a good deal of light on parts of the episode, but in the embittered atmosphere of schismatic politics it is difficult to rely entirely upon the available sources.

It is interesting that when the progressive wing of a later generation of the Irish Republican Brotherhood took control of the organisation in 1912, one of its first actions was to try to preserve the history of the period with which we are concerned. On 26th September, at St. Charles Hotel in Atlantic City, Joseph McGarrity, a Tyrone man whose papers were recently the subject of a series of articles by Sean Cronin in *The Irish Times*, not only reformed the Clan na Gael but also secured a pledge. This was from the veteran Fenians Devoy and Colonel Ricard O'Sullivan Burke who had played a leading part in the events of 1867. At that time they were the only two men alive who had an extensive knowledge of the movement from Fenian times, and they pledged themselves to write their memoirs.

Finally, before turning to the events which culminated in the hangings of the Manchester Martyrs, it is well to recall one quotation:

"Anyone who cares for truth and loves the Irish and will write on history does an immense service to Ireland and England too."[1] An understanding of the tragic events that took place in the streets of Manchester more than a hundred years ago is a service not only to Ireland but to England too.

[1] Frederick York Powell to Mrs. J. R. Green, as quoted in *The Irish Tangle* by Sir Shane Leslie.

I

Kelly and Deasy were their Names

One of the most audacious outrages that have occurred in this
country for many years was perpetrated in open day, within the
limits of the city of Manchester by a party of Irish desperadoes.

In those words, the *Annual Chronicle* of 1867 described the events of
18th September which took place near the railway arch on Hyde Road,
Manchester, not far from the city gaol at Bellevue.

The Fenian Movement which had taken up arms against British rule
in Ireland was spreading its activities to metropolitan Britain, just as
expatriate Algerians a century later were to carry their struggle for
national independence into the streets of metropolitan France. Indeed,
in many respects the Fenians were the forerunners of movements for
national independence which have shaken the world for a century.
Their methods were necessarily those of conspirators; their means of
struggle were those of desperate men, and inevitably involved violence.
Dispersed across the Irish sea, the Atlantic and even the Pacific Oceans,
their organisation spread its activities to the new continents and bit into
the heart of England with frequent "Fenian outrages", culminating in
an abortive rising in Ireland which was a shattering blow for the
movement.

The movement, founded a decade earlier in the United States, owed
the inspiration for its name and formation to John O'Mahony, while
James Stephens, John O'Leary and O'Donovan Rossa were the chief
organisers. It was they who founded its mouthpiece *The Irish People*
in November, 1863. O'Leary was editor, with Charles Joseph Kickham,
Thomas Clarke Luby and Denis Dowling Mulcahy as his chief assistants. It was the famous O'Donovon Rossa who managed and published
the paper. By 1865 they had 100,000 sworn followers and had infil-
trated important sections of the British Army. It is idle to speculate on
what would have been the outcome had they risen in 1865, their most
opportune moment. But by 1867 the authorities were already alerted

and ready to meet the menace. Stephens and John Devoy, his close associate, were arrested before the uprising, the latter having first helped in the remarkable escape of Stephens to Paris under the direction of Colonel Thomas Kelly who was to be a central figure in the Manchester affair. Many leading Fenians such as Luby, O'Leary, Kickham and Rossa were arrested and sentenced to long terms of imprisonment, the latter undergoing the most humiliating tortures before emerging as an almost symbolic figure in the history of Fenianism.

The Irish Republican Brotherhood, as the movement was known in Ireland, was stiffened by many officers who had served with distinction in the American Civil War. Two of them, Colonel Kelly and Captain Deasy, were among those who eluded the police and crossed the Irish Sea to reorganise and raise the morale of the Fenian groups in metropolitan Britain, while Stephens and O'Mahony had met up in Paris.

Both Irish Americans, their accents alone were bound to arouse suspicion—but curiously they were arrested after being seen loitering in the early hours of 11th September, in Oak Street, Shudehill, not far from the centre of Manchester, where they had apparently gone to clear up a complaint by one of the members of the movement. Two of their colleagues managed to escape and at that time the police, unaware of the identity of their captives, merely suspected them of plotting to rob a shop. They were charged under the Vagrancy Act and remanded in custody. Meanwhile, communications with the Irish police revealed their probable identity.

Kelly, who was a native of Mount Bellew in Galway, born in 1833, was a farmer's son. It was intended originally that he should train for the priesthood, but young Kelly was ill-suited for this kind of life and instead became an apprentice in the printing trade in Loughrea. Like so many young Irishmen with ambition and enterprise, he was to leave his impoverished native land for new opportunities across the Atlantic.

In the United States, having been active in the Emmet Monument Association and the New York Printers' Union, he became involved in Fenian activities in its earliest days in 1857, taking the Fenian Oath which bound him in allegiance to the cause:

> I Thomas Kelly in the presence of almighty God do solemnly swear allegiance to the Irish Republic, now virtually established, and that I will do my very utmost, at every risk while life lasts, to defend its independence and integrity; and finally that I will yield

B

implicit obedience, in all things not contrary to the laws of God, to the commands of my superior officers.

By 1867 he himself was a senior officer, having already founded a newspaper in Nashville, Tennessee. Caught up in the civil war, he rose to the rank of Captain, having been severely wounded in the service of the Union forces. For America he fought with great skill and courage, winning rapid promotion; but he was to remain true to his oath of allegiance to Ireland. Thus, although forced to abandon the newspaper when civil war broke out, his service with the 10th Ohio, an Irish Regiment, and his military experience during which he was for a time Chief Signal Officer with General Thomas, were to equip him for the struggle closest to his heart.

At the time when Kelly came to Lancashire, the organisation of the Irish Republican Brotherhood in Great Britain had been placed under the leadership of three other Irish American officers. They were Captain Murphy, in charge of activities in Scotland; Colonel Burke, in charge of Southern England, who was to be involved in the rescue and live to be one of the veteran Fenians of the revival which led to 1916; and Captain O'Meagher Condon, who was to play a leading role in the Manchester affair, in charge of the Northern Counties.

Prior to the arrest, Kelly and Deasy together with Captain Michael O'Brien, soon to be a central and heroic figure in the trials to come, had been staying with Condon in Shudehill. Although this account of the matter is challenged by some of his contemporaries like Neary and even Devoy, it would seem that it was Condon who was responsible for organising the rescue.

In the absence of Stephens, Kelly's position at the centre of the Fenian movement must have been one of the highest responsibility, with *de facto* control of the movement while its official leaders were in exile. His release would be a matter of the utmost urgency to his followers; his incarceration would be another hammer blow that the movement could not afford in the wake of the Irish disaster earlier that year.

In a contemporary account of "the Fenian Outrage"[1] the following assessment was made of Kelly, whose arrest was a major coup for the British authorities:

> Col. Kelly is said to be an Irish American, a man of great talent, and has had considerable military experience, having held commands of importance in the Southern States. He was the trusted

[1] C. G. Smith, loc. cit.

friend and adviser of Stephens when that person was at the head of the Movement, but perhaps the head centre himself had not more influence among the brotherhood or stood higher in the confidence of his countrymen than did Kelly. They had unlimited faith in his integrity; they relied on his military skill for the planning of expeditions that were to be undertaken, and he was consulted in all matters of importance connected with the conspiracy. Not only was he the chief adviser but he was looked upon as the principal fighting man of the Brotherhood and was known among the Fenians by the high sounding title of "Kelly the Soldier". When Stephens [the Fenian leader], was busy in Dublin in perfecting the plan of the Fenians, Kelly was his right-hand man. Stephens was arrested while in the midst of his work, but Kelly succeeded in eluding both spies and detectives. He did not leave Ireland although a price was set upon his head, and it was impossible for him to move about without running the risk of detection. His friend Stephens was in prison and he determined to effect his release. The wonderful manner in which Stephens escaped from Richmond gaol is now a matter of notoriety, and it is also well known that the escape was planned and carried out with much daring by Kelly—Stephens and Kelly left Ireland together. They remained together in Paris for a short time, when Kelly left for America, but returned and again took up his quarters in the French capital. He is said to have opposed the recent rising in Ireland. . . . It was urged by him that the people were not sufficiently prepared and armed to carry out a successful insurrectionary movement, that the arrangements of the Government were so complete that they could crush the rebellion at a single blow, and that the rising at that time would lead to bloodshed and misery, without in any way furthering the cause of the Fenians. This counsel did not prevail.

Smith's account of Kelly's views on the '67 rising would appear to conflict with the fact that it was he who led it; it may, however, merely indicate a difference of view over timing in that the opportune moment had already passed and Kelly understood this. Stephens had been widely criticised for his failure to take the initiative two years earlier when he was urged on by John Devoy. Kelly, Devoy and the Irish American officer pressed Stephens into action while Kelly opposed the ambitious plans of John Devoy. The conflict between the various accounts merely reflects a difference over military tactics, not of principle. While in the United States, Mitchel thought it unwise to fight while Britain was at peace and therefore opposed any rising, preferring to wait, while strongly criticising what he considered to be the make-believe of the Fenian movement. From a purely military point of view he was right, but this split itself weakened the military effectiveness of the Fenian movement.

Indeed, quite apart from Britain's preparedness, tactical splits in the movement in the United States had also weakened it as an effective fighting force. The majority of American members had decided on a remarkably futile venture, dissipating their strength on an ill-conceived attempt to invade Canada.

The price of the '67 uprising was the sentences of twenty years' penal servitude on Luby, O'Leary and Kickham and a life sentence on O'Donovan Rossa. In passing, it should be added that the man who pronounced sentence, Chief Justice William Keogh, himself an Irishman, became a much-hated man in Ireland, while defence Counsel Isaac Butt was to make his name and eventually lead the Irish Parliamentary Party. A mellowed and almost pitiful figure, he succumbed to the soft life of a much-flattered leader of a tame opposition only to fall before the rising star of Charles Stewart Parnell.

Nevertheless, Fenian activity was to continue in England, after a plan to capture Chester Castle had failed miserably because of the notorious spy Corydon who warned the authorities in advance. One of the participants in this abortive attack was the young Michael Davitt, perhaps the greatest and saintliest Irish leader of the century. But if the Chester Castle venture failed it showed that a mass attack by Fenians in England was possible. Until his arrest they could still rely on the able leadership of Kelly. Like Michael Collins half a century later, he had astonished friend and foe alike by his ability to move about Dublin without disguise under the noses of the British for several months, always eluding capture. His capture in Manchester, where there was no suspicion of his presence, was therefore particularly ironical.

Of Deasy less is known, but he was widely described in the British Press as Kelly's *aide-de-camp*. Although less renowned than Kelly, he too had displayed great bravery in battle during the American Civil War, in which he was also wounded. A County Cork man, he was to return to his county in September, 1865. He was soon a marked man and spent a short period in prison before his appearance in Manchester. When Kelly arrived with about 150 Irish American officers in 1867 to help arrange plans for the uprising he was joined by Deasy. It was their common American background revealed in their speech which, more than anything, led to their identity being discovered after their arrest.

After the split in the movement, the Irish-oriented section was little favoured in America. It was known as the "Chatham Street Wing", Colonel W. R. Roberts leading the other grouping. Stephens was not alone in being the object of criticism; Kelly himself was under attack for his position on the '67 rising and estranged from some of the Fenian circles in Dublin. Nevertheless he had been elected "Deputy Central Organiser of the Irish Republic" and in the heart of enemy territory it was his task to keep liaison between headquarters and Manchester under the new arrangement of the Fenian Movement.

Indeed, Kelly had virtually displaced Stephens against whose reluctance to strike in 1865 he had rebelled. Although aligned with Stephens against the American wing of the movement, it was Kelly more than any other leader except Devoy who thirsted for action against the English, writing in *The Irishman* of 1st March, 1866, in optimistic terms: "All is well for Ireland yet. Next Christmas I have confidence I will dine with you as a free and independent citizen of the Irish Republic." His enthusiasm for Stephens' return was later to be matched by his bitterness at Stephens' caution. C. G. Smith's account hardly seems accurate in the light of Desmond Ryan's well-documented description in *The Fenian Chief* of the quarrel which led to Kelly's displacement of his leader and must be taken to allude to the tactical quarrels after the 1865 opportunity was missed. It was Kelly who accused Stephens of cowardice while Stephens called upon the Irish people to follow Kelly's leadership. The revolt went off at half cock with few arms, little money and a fair amount of betrayal. Stephens had remained silent, realising that revolt would mean disaster. But Kelly, the man of action, was there and in command when the disaster happened. If his judgement was in question his courage and military skill were not.

Two other important actors in the drama that was to unfold were Edward O'Meagher Condon who had fought with the famous Irish American Corcoran legion in the American Civil War and who headed the Manchester District, and Captain O'Brien who had served with Ricard O'Sullivan Burke in the civil war and now again in England, and who was eventually to pay for his actions with his life. Burke was recommended by Kelly as the best man to purchase arms in England.

Kelly and Deasy, who had given their names as Martin Williams and

John Whyte, were about to be released by the magistrates when a detective officer decided to apply for their remand on suspicion of connection with the Fenian conspiracy. But the news of their arrest and of the arrangements for their transport was filtered out to Fenian sympathisers among the Irish population of Manchester.

More than a tenth of the population of Manchester at that time was Irish, living in areas that resembled the ghettos of North American cities today, and often known as "Little Ireland". In Little Ireland, Engels had observed, "the Irish have discovered the minimum necessities of life, and are now making the English workers acquainted with it". It was among these teeming wretched streets that the news of Kelly's and Deasy's arrest was to pass from mouth to mouth, and among them there lived many ready to join in any attempt to rescue their leaders.

Edward O'Meagher Condon and Michael O'Brien had, of course, worked closely with Kelly, and there is little doubt that he was also well known to a young man called William Philip Allen who lived in Manchester at that time. There were to be no Corydons to warn the authorities of the audacious plan they were to hatch, together with their comrades from "Little Ireland," cemented together by their common nationality and the possession of a common religious background in the Catholic Church, to release the man who himself had been doing the same for his leader James Stephens a few months earlier. Condon, in a remarkable account of the rescue to be published in the *Irish World* of 4th January, 1908, was particularly bitter about the circumstances of the arrest, and its background:

> After the failure of the intended rising in Ireland in 1867 some of us who had gone over there from this side felt that in order to avert danger from friends whose hospitality to us would expose them to severe penalty, we should go to England, where observation was not so close, and await further developments. We had determined not to come home without making, if possible, another effort for Ireland's independence. On going to Manchester, I found Captain O'Rourke, an old comrade of the Corcoran legion during the Civil War, in charge of the National Organisation in Northern England. It was then arranged that he should come back here, and endeavour to secure, if possible, sufficient resources to enable us to begin practical operations.
>
> This was done. Captain James Murphy, formerly of the 20th

Mass., was then in charge of the body in Scotland, and Col. R. Burke in control of the men of the South of England. Captain Deasy, formerly of the 9th Mass, was living in Manchester. He was a splendid soldier, but his retiring disposition rendered him indisposed to take part in the work of organisation. At the Convention there were present nearly sixty delegates from my district. Captain Murphy brought twelve with him from Scotland. No delegates accompanied Colonel Burke. The proceedings were entirely harmonious and satisfactory, and at the close of the Convention everything seemed encouraging and hopeful. . . .

I was entrusted with the control of the Organisation in that section, and from that time until I was captured, I travelled almost constantly through the entire district between the Black Country and the Tyneside. There were many difficulties and embarrassments to overcome. We were receiving no financial aid from America, many good Nationalists had become doubtful of success, many circles were disorganised and some disbanded, and there was no systematic communication between the different branches. In Manchester the organisation had become so weakened that it seemed proper to reduce the number of circles from nine to three. By dint, however, of incessant exertion I had within a few months effected a complete reorganisation throughout the district, and then, in order to inspire the members with renewed confidence and take concerted measures for the future, I recommended to Colonel Kelly, who was at the head of the I.R.B., that a convention of delegates from the whole Organisation throughout Britain be held without delay.

I was walking down a street in Manchester one night in September of the year mentioned, and unarmed, when I saw approaching from the opposite direction two tall men, evidently Irish peelers, with a small individual between them. I stepped aside in order to observe them without being noticed, and, as they came closer, recognised the middle party as Corydon, the informer.

Retracing my steps, I followed the three, meeting with a friend on the way who came with me, and saw that they entered a police station not far off. Warrants were out, we knew, for the arrest of the Irish-Americans who were believed to be still in Britain or Ireland, and it was evident that Corydon had come to assist the police in ferreting out those who were supposed to be in Manchester.

On the next morning I despatched messengers to various points throughout the city to make known the fact that the informer was in town and likely to visit his old resorts, sending William Melvin to notify, among others, Bolger, or O'Bolger, who was sub-centre. When Melvin returned he told me that on going into Bolger's house he found several people there, and that being in a hurry to proceed further, and deeming it difficult to convey the information without attracting attention, he had gone to this man's brother, who lived next door, and given him my message. Bolger seemed to regard Melvin's omission to communicate with him directly as an intentional slight—there had been, I believe, some friction between them—and he came to me later, protesting against Melvin's action, and demanding that he be allowed to make a complaint about it to Colonel Kelly.

Under ordinary circumstances I would not have heeded this childish demand, but just then there were in the city or vicinity some envoys from the Roberts party of the F.B. who had been endeavouring to induce the organisation in Britain to unite with them. I had refused to think of severing relations with the men on this side, who had always clung to the policy of fighting in Ireland, but the Roberts people had succeeded in getting a few men to confer with him on the subject during one of my frequent absences while organising, though without persuading their hearers to take their side.

I was naturally anxious to preserve peace and unity in our ranks and prevent anything like a split among the men whom I was working so hard to keep together. Under these circumstances I assented to Bolger's demand, and requested Colonel Kelly to hear what he had to say. I instructed the three centres and their sub-centres to meet on the next night at a place indicated.

I had, however, previously arranged to organise a circle down in the Black Country on that night, and as, if I failed to keep my appointment, the proposed new members might not come together again, it was absolutely necessary to fulfil that engagement.

The three centres and the other officers met with Colonel Kelly and Captain Deasy, who accompanied him. Bolger's complaint was listened to. Melvin told of the instructions I had given him, proving that no slight was intended, and at the close of the meeting Kelly and Deasy went to a house in Shudehill Market, where I had formerly lodged and where communications were still received, in order to get any of these that might have arrived.

Soon after leaving the house—a little before midnight—they were arrested. Thus did a silly display of wounded vanity lead to the arrest of the head of the organisation and his friend, and the death or incarceration of as brave men as ever pledged their devotion to the cause of Irish liberty.

As Condon's account of the arrest and subsequently of the rescue is the most comprehensive in existence it is reproduced almost in its entirety. But one difficulty for the historian in making an assessment of this version of the events is that it was published in polemical style in answer to some alleged misrepresentations in America by a man called Bolger or O'Bolger who was Condon's deputy in 1867. Devoy was one of Condon's critics and attributed the rescue attempt to the leadership of Burke. This view has been accepted by Desmond Ryan in his Biography of James Stephens as well as in *The Phoenix Flame* and by Dr. F. S. L. Lyons in a lecture reproduced in Moody's collection, *The Fenian Movement*. All these authorities give cause for concern at Condon's account; but the probability is that they are based on Devoy's own account, and his longevity and papers have combined, perhaps, to give undue weight to his description of this particular incident. More likely, Burke gave the orders, including one that no life was to be taken unless it was imperative for the success of the rescue, and Condon was in charge of the actual operation. Nevertheless the reader must be circumspect. Another participant in the affair, Neary, claimed credit for the plan. Condon was concerned to answer what he considered "untruthful and malicious rumours", but his publication contains a unique and graphic account not only of the events leading to the arrests of Kelly and Deasy but, as will be seen, of the later planning of the rescue and its aftermath. It should also be borne in mind that he was writing of events that took place more than forty years earlier and doubtless one cannot rely on every detail, but there seems to be no reason to doubt the circumstances in which he describes how Kelly and Deasy were picked up by the police, however anxious he may have been to place the blame on Bolger.

Devoy's Postbag[1] reveals John Devoy's antagonism to Condon in the period following Condon's release from prison. This was one of the many splits and controversies that characterised latter day Fenianism in

[1] *Devoy's Postbag: 1871–1928*; William O'Brien and Desmond Ryan, Vol. II, 1880–1923, pp. 386–9.

the United States, where Condon was known for his remarkable oratory. Devoy's own "recollections" echoed the charge against Condon; and the flames were fanned by Condon's support for the Irish Parliamentary Party, on which account Devoy sought to give credit for the rescue to Colonel Ricard O'Sullivan Burke. Yet there seems little doubt that Condon had done most of the organisation by the time Burke arrived on the scene. Devoy's own recollections concede that he obtained the history in January, 1871, when he landed at Boston. He alleges that Kelly and Deasy were returning from Condon's court-martial when arrested. He agreed that Peter Rice, "a very small, but sturdy Dublin man . . . who lived many years in New York and died in his native city", fired the fatal shot. Nevertheless, he adamantly declared Condon's claim to leadership to be "absurd".

On 14th January, 1910, John T. Ryan repeated the charge against Condon, accusing him of being a deserter from the Union Army and saying that this was the reason for the refusal of the American authorities to intercede on his behalf. Since the American authorities did intercede and there is no evidence from any other source, it is curious that this accusation should be made in 1910. Ryan must have been acting on hearsay, since he wrote "as I understand it" prefacing the accusation that Condon was entrusted with bringing tools, failed to do so and therefore caused the deaths of Allen, Larkin and O'Brien. The accusation went further in alleging that "Condon failed to appear at the appointed place with the tools or the money, that he was late reaching there, and that he made one or two efforts to depart from the scene before the rescue took place, but was brought back on each occasion on the threat of death. I further understand that he secreted the funds and the tools in a chest in his room at the house where he was boarding, and that as a matter of fact he had not been near that place the night before the rescue at all." He further accuses him on the basis of hearsay of revealing this evidence to the police, and asks John Devoy to "straighten him out" if he is wrong on any of these points. All the evidence from the trial—Condon had £8 in his pocket when arrested—and both Burke's and Denvir's testimony that O'Brien and Burke spent the night with Condon planning the operation tends to exculpate Condon, and it may well have been the defence alibis which led to these hearsay accusations. Their date and foundation seems to indicate that they have little substance.

Devoy's recollections quote a letter from Ricard O'Sullivan Burke naming the men who volunteered for the rescue—"James Lavery,

John Neary, Thomas O'Bolger, Peter Ryan, William Melvin, Michael Larkin, Timothy Featherstone, Charles Moorehouse, Peter Rice, William Philip Allen, Patrick Bloomfield, John Stoneham, Joseph Keeley, John Ryan, James Cahill, and the two American Officers, Michael O'Brien and O'Meagher Condon".

He claimed that he had selected Thomas O'Bolger and Peter Ryan to undertake the extra hazardous duty, and advised the conduct at and after the rescue, in particular that no life was to be taken unless necessary to the success of the rescue, when it was to be taken without an instant's hesitation.

But again, Burke concedes that he only dealt with the Manchester men through an intermediary and relied on a report of the rescue made by O'Bolger to him some years afterwards. Condon was to provide "everything necessary to get our officers quickly out of the van and into our own hands, and to see them away to a place or places of security". In itself, this shows Condon in a central role.

O'Brien was to cover the retreat, presumably one of the reasons for his capture. He names James Cahill as killing one of the horses and commends Lavery, O'Bolger, Ryan, Rice and Cahill for their energetic action. This is hardly surprising in view of the source of his report. Burke drove near to the scene in a cab after the event and was modest enough to say that the credit was due only to the Manchester I.R.B. "who actually accomplished it", adding "I only gave form and direction to that force".[1]

There is nothing of substance in his account to provide a basis for Devoy's harsh view, other than O'Bolger's account upon which all the others up to the present day have been founded.

In any event, the result was that after their identification Kelly and Deasy were to be removed to Bellevue Gaol on the other side of the City for their remand. Telegrams from Dublin Castle and the Home Office warned the magistrates of a possible attempt to release them, and it still remains a mystery why greater precautions were not taken by the authorities in Manchester. Nevertheless some extra precautions were in fact taken and the two men were conveyed in a sort of Victorian Black Maria—a horse-drawn prison van driven by a policeman. Police Constables Shaw and Yarwood with Detectives Bromley and Taylor were positioned on the box; Constables Knox and Connell were behind.

Inside the van was another officer holding the keys. This was the ill-

[1] See Devoy's *Recollections*, Chapters XXXV and XXXVI.

fated Sergeant Charles Brett, a dedicated and courageous police officer with a reputation for humanity and honesty among those in his charge, who frequently referred to him informally as "Charlie". Although it should no doubt have been anticipated that a police officer would ride inside the van to survey the prisoners, Condon accepts that this was not foreseen.

The van was in effect a portable prison, divided into two rows of cells by a corridor and only very dimly lit through overhead ventilators and the grating on the door. The seven guards surprisingly carried no arms and were equipped only with staves, while the keys to the van were carried inside by Sergeant Brett who alone could give access to the prisoners or allow their release.

A number of prisoners were being transported in the van, but Kelly and Deasy were kept handcuffed in separate compartments, unable to communicate with one another. Behind the van there followed a cab containing more policemen. Their additional presence was obviously dictated by the importance of their charges Kelly and Deasy, not by the occupants of the other cells which housed three women and a boy being taken to a reformatory. Their route took them outside the centre of the City along the straight road to the gaol over which passed a railway arch immortalised in contemporary engravings of the amazing scene that was to follow.

Meanwhile, at a carefully chosen spot close to the arch an unexpected reception was awaiting the van—a reception composed of Fenians, with arms purchased at Birmingham, who were to give the arch the name of "The Fenian Arch" in the folklore of Manchester. When the comfortable gentlemen of London opened up their copies of *The Times* on the morning of Thursday, 19th September, 1867, this was what they read on page 7 about the "smashing of the van":

> Wednesday, 9 o'clock
> This morning the supposed Colonel Kelly and Captain Deasy, having been remanded by the Magistrates, were placed in a cell with a view to removal to the city gaol, Bellevue. About 3 o'clock the van was drawn up in front of the police court to remove all the prisoners to gaol and among them the two Fenians. At this time the police noticed two men hanging about whom they suspected to be Fenians, and a policeman made a rush at one of them to arrest him, in which he succeeded, but not till the man had drawn a dagger and attempted to stab him. The blow was avoided. The

other suspected person made his escape. In consequence of this Kelly and Deasy were put in irons before being taken to the van. When the van left the city it had to proceed over Ardwick Green and along Hyde Road, a fine open street leading to the gaol, and nearly a mile in length; it was drawn by two horses and was guarded behind by seven policemen. The van had proceeded about half a mile up this road when on passing under the viaduct which carries the London and North Western Railway across, with an open field on the right, a volley of shots were fired at it. The policemen not seeing where the shots came from, dropped off the van and spread themselves out wide. There was a rush of 30 to 40 Irishmen upon the police and upon the van. One man had a hatchet, another a hammer, and a third a bayonet with which they set to work to break open the van. One man took a revolver and fired into the lock. Ultimately men with large stones—one of them nearly 100 lb weight—broke through the top of the van and the panels of the door behind, and set all the prisoners including the Fenians at liberty. The policemen collected in a body and made a rush to prevent the prisoners being liberated but several revolvers were discharged among them, and one constable was shot over one of his eyes, causing his eye to protrude, and was taken to the infirmary. A young man, a bystander, was shot through the head. It is expected the Fenians, being in irons, will be recaptured. The streets of Manchester have been in a state of great excitement all the evening. The officer shot in the head is Sgt. Brett. The ball passed through his head and lodged in his hat. William O'Meara Allen, said to have fired the fatal shot, was chased and taken. Detective Bromley received a shot in one of his thighs. Another policeman was shot in his back, wounded but slightly. Both the horses in the van were shot. The driver was knocked off his box with a stone. A dozen arrests have been made. The two Fenians are at liberty, but a squadron of Dragoons are passing the Telegraph Office, guarding a carriage, at this moment, which may contain further important captives.

The inside story of the rescue was not to appear in print until Condon published his account and must be read in the light of the circumstances in which it was published. It is clear that it had been alleged by Condon's critics and accepted by many historians that the tools for breaking open the van had been forgotten. Even if this were so Condon denied any responsibility on his part and the whole argument was inflated beyond its importance in view of the remarkable success of the assailants. While it would be rash to accept any one version of the event, as one picks ones way through the evidence it is clear from *The Times* report that some makeshift tools were certainly used in addition to the large stones and rocks, for the report referred to "hatchets", "a hammer", and "a bayonet". Whether these were the products of private enterprise on the part of individuals or distributed according to a preconceived plan one cannot know, but the whole atmosphere of urgency and a situation which called for on-the-spot decisions and individual initiative as well as organisation and leadership must inevitably lead to confusion. Whatever the accuracy of the following account given by Condon, the result was a startling success and a severe blow to the prestige of the English authorities which they could not forgive.

When I returned on the following morning [11th September], I found that Kelly and Deasy were in prison, and bitterly regretted that I had allowed them to be drawn from their seclusion for the petty cause above indicated. No lawyer had been secured to defend them, but they were remanded for a week, and this gave me time to make preparations to release them. I sent word to the three centres—Nolan, Neary and Lavery—to meet me at the house of the former that night, and when we met, expressed my determination to rescue my friends if possible.

If any of these centres had received any note or message from anyone bearing on this subject, he failed to mention it, and under the circumstances he wasn't likely to forget anything of the kind. All present favoured an attempt at release, but Nolan strongly urged that I should procure men for the work from other cities, to which they would depart when it was accomplished. I thought that it would be a slight on the Manchester men to ask others to take their places in an affair of the sort, and it was soon decided that they only should participate.

I had planned a somewhat similar release of prisoners on a former occasion. When it was proposed to seize the Island of Campobello in 1866, I was directed to bring to that point or to Eastport, near it, a body of men from Canada. Some accompanied me by the Suspension Bridge route, while a number of others from Toronto, in order not to attract attention, proceeded by way of Montreal. These were, however, arrested at Cornwall and imprisoned. When the movement referred to failed of success, I determined, if possible, to effect the liberation of my friends, and going to Toronto, whither it was reported they would be brought for trial, I planned to intercept the prison van as it proceeded from the gaol to the court-house at the bridge over the River Don, and set free the prisoners.

The arranged plan was not, however, carried out, because the Fenians were never brought up for trial. They were held in Cornwall for several months, and finally succeeded in tunnelling under the prison, the surrounding yard and the outside wall, and one stormy night they passed out safely, secured a boat on the river shore, and crossed over to the American side—to freedom.

In Manchester the conditions were somewhat similar. The van which conveyed prisoners to the gaol had to pass under the arch of a railroad bridge on Hyde Road, beside which was a vacant lot, whence egress could be had to the railroad yard and the country beyond. When I enquired of the centres what resources were available, I found that, except one pound, held by Nolan, there were no funds in the possession of the Manchester Circle, nor any revolvers. This was certainly a very unsatisfactory state of affairs, but it had to be dealt with.

While organising through the country I had directed the circles to retain their funds until urgently needed, though this system was different from that in vogue before my arrival. Its propriety, however, was made evident on this occasion. When I visited the circles near by, the money asked for was forthcoming at once, and when more was needed a messenger carrying my written request was promptly furnished with the funds required.

I visited the caterer allowed to supply meals to the prisoners in Bellevue, where Kelly and Deasy were confined, and arranged to have them furnished with regular meals, and then went to secure the services of a lawyer for my friends, seeking first Ernest Jones, the famous Chartist leader, who was then practising law in Manchester. He informed me that under the English system, the counsel had to receive briefs from a solicitor, and recommended me to secure one of these, named Nuttall, whom I requested to visit the prisoners, and he did so.

It was, of course, necessary to have arms, and I despatched William Darragh to Birmingham to purchase ten revolvers, in order to avoid any suspicions which might be excited through an attempt to buy them in Manchester. I had decided also to take Kelly and Deasy, when released, first to Ashton-under-Lyne to obtain a change of clothing and other disguises, and then convey them to Newcastle, or an adjacent town, whence we could procure passage to some Continental port. It was expected that Corydon would be brought to Manchester to identify the prisoners, and for several days before I had sent parties to the railroad depots to watch for his arrival. [Corydon was the notorious renegade who acted as stool pigeon for the authorities in various Fenian trials.]

Within a few days I felt satisfied that, if the necessary secrecy was maintained, success would attend our efforts. When all arrangements were practically completed, in order not to leave the organisation without a head during my absence or in the possible case of my capture, I wired Captain Murphy and Colonel Burke to come to Manchester, so that they might fill my place.

Kelly had passed for my uncle at the house where he stopped, and my message merely said: "Uncle is dying, come immediately", signing the name which I employed in correspondence with those addressed. Captain Burke was then absent from Glasgow organising as usual, and didn't get my telegram till too late, but Colonel Burke received the message sent him, and reached Manchester on the day before the affair took place. It was not necessary for him to do anything but wait, and he took no part in the rescue.

I had selected the spot for stopping the van several days before. It was, in fact, so evidently the most suitable one that no man, unless he was blind, could select another for our purpose. I have learned that privately it has been said that Colonel Burke was telegraphed for because there was some doubt of my ability to manage the affair.

Now I never knew that—except one other—anyone but myself knew the Colonel's address, or that of Captain Murphy, and I don't believe that anyone ever spent even the cost of a telegram for any purpose connected with the rescue unless I supplied him with the money. If it were deemed necessary that Colonel Burke should take charge of the affair why should he remain miles away, in the other end of the city, while the rescue was taking place, though he had seen Kelly and Deasy carried off in the van to Bellevue prison?

Captain O'Brien was also absent, but through inadvertence; and I only of the American officers was present at, and took part in, the release of the prisoners.

THE PRISONERS ARE CONVEYED TO BELLEVUE JAIL

HYDE ROAD (BELLEVUE) PRISON

THE RESCUE OF THE LEADERS

COLONEL KELLY

THE VAN

SERGEANT BRETT

Darragh reached Manchester on the evening of the 17th with the arms which I had sent him to purchase, and Colonel Burke and Captain O'Brien came with me to the place where I distributed them in accordance with the recommendations of the centres, who, of course, knew more about the qualities of their men that I or any other stranger could possibly know.

Some of those named in the statement by Bolger as being among the men who received arms from me were not present on the occasion, and some of the names given belonged to those who took no part in the transaction, while others, actually present, are omitted.

One of these was Daniel Reddin of Dublin, one of the bravest and coolest men I have ever met. He was arrested after the rescue, in which he had done his whole duty, and suffered five years' penal servitude, but became paralysed in prison from punishment, while the alleged doctors pretended to believe that he was shamming, and prodded the soles of the helpless man's feet with large needles. He died soon after his release.

One of those whom Bolger mentioned as a participant, a man named P. Hoey, requested me to speak with him privately when we were ready to leave the place where I had distributed the arms. He was very nervous, affected to consider himself liable to immediate arrest, and was anxious to get away from the city as soon as possible. He urgently demanded money to enable him to do so, and as it would be positively dangerous to have him remain near us, I gave him the half-sovereign that he required, and felt relieved when he started off.

On that occasion I gave Bolger money to pay for a cab in which he was to proceed to the Hyde Road Bridge when the prisoners were placed in the van, and notify us of their coming. I also gave a man, named Brannon, money to hire another cab, which he was to take to a certain point on the Ashton Road, and there wait for Kelly, Deasy and myself.

He paid the cabman, but didn't go with him, and, as might be expected, there was no cab waiting when looked for. Brannon was arrested later, and served five years in penal servitude.

After I had distributed the arms, Colonel Burke and Captain O'Brien returned with me to my lodgings. The next morning O'Brien accompanied me to a house on Oldham Road, where the intended rescuers were to gather, while Colonel Burke went to the

Police Court. I never met him again till I reached New York from Portland Prison eleven years later.

The men selected, ten in number, assembled promptly at the place indicated. Before they started for Hyde Road I distributed some money among them, and directed them to keep off the street and escape observation as much as possible. There were several saloons in the vicinity into which they could go.

Just before this, however, I received a note from Nuttall, the solicitor, informing me that Ernest Jones had left for Glasgow on the previous night, he having agreed some time before to engage in a public discussion with Professor Blackie of Edinburgh. He had, it appeared, forgotten that date when he undertook to plead for my friends. I had then to visit Nuttall and arrange with him as quickly as possible to procure other counsel, giving him, of course, the necessary fee, after which I hastened to the scene of the proposed rescue.

On arriving there I was surprised to see a number of men standing in groups on the sidewalk, while a group of Englishmen on the opposite side of the street were observing them closely. There had evidently been culpable leakage, for we could only hope to effect our purpose by keeping the authorities off their guard, and I wanted none on the ground but those who were armed and could protect themselves, as well as effect the release of our friends.

I gave some of these men money to take the others into the saloons near, and keep them from attracting attention. At this time Neary came to me on the sidewalk and told me that he felt ill, and would be unable to use the revolver which I had given him the night before, handing it back to me at the same time. He then promptly went home, but there was no delay or difficulty in finding another to take and use the weapon. Bolger's assertion that Neary was one of those who kept the crowd at bay when the prisoners were released, and formed one of what he calls the "rear guard", is simply absurd. Neary left the ground half an hour at least before Kelly and Deasy were taken out.

But not only was information of the intended attack communicated to many men, but some women were also made aware of it, and as a result three of these came along Hyde Road a short time previous to the van's arrival. In order to get them away from the scene before anything unpleasant happened, O'Brien invited them to a restaurant some distance up the road, and while he was there the stoppage of the van and the release of the prisoners was effected. He only reached the scene just as they were taken out.

Something has been said about the failure to provide tools to open the van, and it has been alleged that I was instructed to bring these to the spot. Now, considering that I was in charge of the whole business, had to make all the preparations, give all the necessary instructions, and provide the funds to carry them out, and attend personally to almost all details, even to furnishing the prisoners with proper food, and that I had arranged to escort them to a place of safety, and get them out of the country, it seems absurd to suppose that some unnamed or unknown party would undertake to give me instructions to do something which scores could, and would have been quite ready to do, if the possibility of its necessity had been suggested. I had freely given money for everything required until I had only about forty dollars left to pay the fares and expenses of Kelly, Deasy and myself to the North, and would, of course, without a moment's hesitation, have given whatever sum was required to bring to the Hyde Road Bridge anything that might be needed. I was a stranger, and had to trust to those belonging to the city for information with regard to the manner in which prisoners were conveyed to the gaol, and all with whom I conferred about the matter assured me that invariably only one or two officers accompanied the van, and that the man in charge, who had the keys, always stood on the step in the rear outside.

It appeared, then, only necessary after stopping the van to take the keys from this man, and release the prisoners. If the authorities became aware of our project, or suspected that one was on foot, they would undoubtedly have sent a cavalry escort to guard the prisoners on their way to the gaol, and our hopes of effecting a rescue would be frustrated. It appears clearly evident that until a fuss occurred at the van door, to which I will refer presently, there was not the slightest suspicion in the minds of the authorities that any interference whatever would be attempted with the van.

When the examination of the prisoners was concluded at the Courthouse, they were again remanded to Bellevue, Kelly on the testimony of an inspector from Scotland Yard, and Deasy on that of an official from Dublin. Evidently rumours of an intention to effect a rescue had been heard in certain quarters, notwithstanding all my efforts to preserve secrecy, for groups of people gathered around the van when the prisoners were being placed in it, and one of them drew a long knife, and muttered some threatening words. The police promptly seized the idiot who had the weapon, and threw him into the van with the other prisoners. This incident evidently alarmed the court officers, and induced them to send four men in a cab behind the van, which carried six more, while the policeman who had charge of the conveyance stood inside instead of outside, as he had invariably done before. Not one of these policemen was, however, armed, a fact which proved that the officials had no suspicion whatever that a rescue would be attempted.

This talk about failure to provide tools for opening the van door, which no one actually engaged doubted could and would be opened without difficulty, is simply a display of "backstairs wit", the criticism of those who are always wise after the event; which had its origin three thousand miles away from the scene, and emanated from those paid to propagate slanders against men who have done their whole duty under all circumstances and at all times. The object, in fact, of these malicious statements must be clear to anyone possessed of more than the feeble intelligence of a brute.

Bolger proceeded to the scene in a cab, which I furnished him with the money to provide, and signalled to us, as directed, that the prisoners were coming. But instead of holding the horse when he got out, in order to prevent the cabman from driving to Belle-vue, and notifying the prison warders, he let him go, and the driver promptly hastened to the prison, and gave the alarm to the officials, with the result that eight warders, some of whom came in the cab, hurried to the scene as fast as possible. These were the only ones who gave us any trouble. It was they who captured Allen, Larkin and O'Brien. The policemen who accompanied the van were a miscellaneous lot, apparently embracing the long and short and the fat and lean of the Manchester force, and they were utterly helpless to make any resistance against us. The van was stopped, the off-horse shot, and the other held as soon as the conveyance reached the vacant lot beyond the bridge.

The policemen sprang off, appeared dazed, and hastened out of range as soon as possible, and though some of the English crowd which gathered threw stones, not one of our men was touched. Lavery, the only centre present, sought to break in the roof with a large stone, but, this method involved too much delay, Rice fired at the lock, and just at this moment the officer in charge, who had been crouching down, raised his head to look through the louvres of the ventilator in the door, and received a bullet wound which proved fatal. The keys were then handed out by one of the ordinary prisoners, and the door opened. If those keys had not been promptly forthcoming, some scaffold poles lying near an adjacent house would have been used to batter in the door. The prisoners were both handcuffed when released. On seeing this I ran into a house and got some knives, with which, using a brick for a hammer, I attempted to cut the links of Deasy's handcuffs. They were too strong, however, and I then told him and Kelly to start off, saying that we would keep the crowd back, until they were at a safe distance. We then followed. At this time friends and foes were mixed, all running towards the wall, and getting over it at various points. When we reached and crossed it, a train coming in from somewhere passed slowly across the route which the released men had taken, and cut us off from them. Brennan, however, knew the locality, and guided me to the house of a friend some distance off, where I exchanged my coat and hat for others, cut off my moustache, and then, notwithstanding the urgent remonstrances of Brennan, started out again to go to the house in Ashton to which I had arranged that Kelly and Deasy were to be conveyed when rescued. I wanted to hire a cab to take me as quickly as possible, and Nugent brought me to a livery stable in the vicinity. We found, however, that the news of the rescue had spread all over the town, and when I asked the fare to Ashton, those in the stable regarded us with suspicion, and became so inquisitive that I felt sure we would be followed if we hired a conveyance there. Then, affecting to regard the fare demanded as too high, and saying that any other day would do as well for the journey, I left with my companion.

What had occurred in the stable seemed to make him somewhat apprehensive, and he frequently turned round to see if we were being followed. His movements attracted the attention of a detective and some others when we were crossing Oldham Road. These trailed us, finally coming up close behind. I turned and faced them, demanding why they followed us, and they stepped back and shouted out to the passers-by to aid them in our arrest. There was evidently nothing left but to escape if possible, but when I turned again I found that Nugent had disappeared.

Knowing nothing of the locality I rushed up what appeared to be a street, but proved to be only a blind alley with no outlet. When I started back to make my way out the crowd gave way, but a detective struck me on the head with a heavy club, and this brought me to my knees for an instant. Rising, however, again I pushed on, tearing myself loose from those who tried to grab me, until I came to a narrow bridge crossing a canal. Here, among others, there were planted in my path two big, half-drunken women, who flung themselves on me, locking their arms around my neck, as if I were their long-lost brother. I had never tackled a proposition of that kind before, and no time was allowed me to consider how to deal with it. The detectives and mob closed in, and, after being badly battered on the head, I was seized and over-powered. Some human being among the horde of brutes ventured to expostulate at my treatment, and one man called out: "Don't murder him". But this unfortunate party was quickly hammered into silence, and fastened to me with a handcuff. Then I was dragged to a police station in the vicinity and thrown into a cell. Meanwhile other incidents proper to note here had occurred in the field between Hyde Road and the railroad yard. Kelly and Deasy were safely on their way to Ashton, and the rescuers and the mob were scattered over the ground, all running towards the wall.

Among these was Larkin, who had a short time before returned from the funeral of his father in Ireland, bringing with him his feeble old mother. He had been stricken down on his return with a severe illness, and had only been able to get out of bed a few days before. He could hardly walk, and O'Brien and Allen helped him along as best they could; but in consequence of the delay which this involved all three were soon surrounded, and, led by the warders from Bellevue, brought down by the cabman who drove Bolger to the ground, the mob seized Larkin first and when Allen and O'Brien tried to rescue him, the latter was knocked down by a brick, and Allen was overpowered a moment later. The story as told by Bolger, to the effect that he, while escaping over the wall, had a hold of Larkin, and that O'Brien was then on the wall, is without a shadow of foundation in fact.

Soon after I had been put in the police cell, Allen, Larkin, and O'Brien were brought in. We were all pretty badly battered, and, as a woman who was among those brought to identify us later remarked, "were perfect sights". Many others picked up all over the city were brought in all through the night and thrown into our cell, until it was packed with men as closely as that other English prison, known as the "Black Hole of Calcutta" was on a former noted occasion.

I was surprised and shocked to see Larkin there. On account of his weakness, he had gone into a saloon near the bridge, and sat down quietly, waiting until the van came up. He was unarmed, and had I noticed him I would at once have sent him home. He said to me in the cell that he ought not to have been required to take part in the rescue; and when I asked him how he came to be there, he replied that Bolger had gone to him, told him that he must take part, and when he pleaded he was sick and had a large family to care for, Bolger declared that if he failed to be present he would be disgraced, and regarded as a coward for ever. "I thought", the poor fellow added, "that it was your orders, otherwise I would never have gone."

As the news began to filter in and eye witnesses gave their own version of the story, the details began to emerge more clearly. No details were given in the first reports concerning the death of Sgt. Brett. The implication was that a shot was fired at the lock, not at Brett, but already a presumption of guilt was established against Allen. Before any legal proceedings *The Times* felt able to say: "Allen is said to have acted as Captain of the rescuing party and had been waiting with a number of followers for hours before the van arrived. He shot at the door and policemen on the box and at the horses shooting one through the head. He also fired at Brett who was inside the van and tumbled out when the door was forced."

Whatever view one may take of this shooting of an invisible target, in one vital respect at least the forecast of *The Times* was inaccurate— in spite of their being in irons the two Fenian chiefs were never recaptured. Speculation in the press as to their whereabouts continued for weeks. A chain of friendly hands spirited them away in spite of the strenuous efforts of the police.

The police suspected that Kelly and Deasy were hidden in Ancoats, regarded as the Fenian district of Manchester. Several anonymous letters were received by the Mayor, one of them alleging that the fugitives were in a house at Evey Street, Ancoats. At 11.30 a.m. fifty constables arrived at the house. The shutters were drawn and an eager crowd watched with excitement as the police surrounded the house, armed with Colt revolvers. Two City Magistrates, Messrs. Kennedy and Clarke, accompanied them and Inspector Garner ordered the door to be burst open. Only one man and two women were in the house, but there was some evidence that it had been occupied by others who had probably made a hasty retreat leaving behind correspondence and papers connected with the Dublin conspiracy. Several hats of different sizes, Irish newspapers and a portrait of Stephens were the police's only haul; of the wanted men, there was no trace.

The last that was seen of Deasy after the two parted company at Taylor Street was when he entered a house in Beswick, still handcuffed, and emerged with another man, the handcuffs having been struck off with a hatchet upon the sink stone in the kitchen. The lady of the house identified the stranger as speaking with an American accent. He left at 4.20 p.m. along Wellington Road towards Bradford, Manchester. Allen ensured Kelly's escape before falling into the hands of the pursuing mob.

A £300 reward was offered for information leading to the capture of the two fugitives who were described in the following terms:

> Colonel Thomas J. Kelly, aged 36, 5' 6", hair (cropped close) whiskers, and beard brown, eyes hazel, flat nose (large nostrils) stout build, one tooth deficient next to double one in right top side, scar over right temple, small scar inside of right arm, large scar on inside of belly from an ulcerated wound. Dress brown mixture suit, coat (with pockets at sides) deerstalker hat.
> Captain Timothy Deasy, age 29, height 5' 10", complexion swarthy, eyes hazel, hair and moustache dark brown, whiskers shaved, of proportionate build, long face, sickly appearance, speaks with strong American accent. Dress dark pea jacket, dark grey trousers, deerstalker hat.

On 24th September it was reported in one of the Liverpool evening papers that two men closely resembling Kelly and Deasy had entered Liverpool on foot while the detectives were watching railway stations and had succeeded in getting on board the *Hibernia* (appropriately named) and leaving for America. There was some speculation as to whether they would be arrested at Londonderry.

On the 26th a man called Clinton claimed to have seen Kelly making for the Irish quarter of Nottingham. On 1st October a Scotsman was roused from his bed by the Mayor of Bristol, suspected of being Deasy.

On 14th November *The Times* reported that "Deasy is said to have crossed the Atlantic in the *City of Paris*, joining the ship at Liverpool and being assisted by Kelly who was disguised as a porter." On 15th November it was reported from "reliable sources" that Kelly was in Belgium. Summing up the speculation one contemporary writer (C. G. Smith) wrote: "It has been hinted as is feared, that they are both across the wide Atlantic Ocean or have escaped to France."

It should be added as a postscript that Kelly was lucky to escape from the van with his life, a shot having passed through the van four inches from his head. But even this should throw some light on the circumstances in which Sgt. Brett met with his unfortunate and tragic death. The poignancy of the drama lay not so much in the daring rescue as in the events which were to follow as Imperial Britain prepared to make an example of those unwise enough to challenge her authority in Ireland and take up arms against her laws. As the police combed out the Irish quarter of Manchester for suspects, Kelly and Deasy were making their way to freedom.

It was reported by the *New York Irish People* on 16th November that Captain Deasy had arrived in New York.

On 30th November, 1867, the following letter published in *The Irish People* was reported by the *Freeman's Journal*.

Sept. 21, 1867

My Dear.... I have arrived here safely, *and here I intend to remain.* To obtain liberty for a people, risks and sacrifices are necessary. I am willing to take my share. The devotion of those around me proves their earnestness in the same direction. With that never ceasing hope of freedom beyond, we can bear to struggle on for a great cause, trusting to posterity to do us justice in our efforts to obtain liberty. ... You know how we stand here. If Irishmen in America but do their duty, we shall not be wanting in ours when the day of trial comes, the machination of some who must still insist on raising the *slogan* of party to the contrary notwithstanding. This is not the place to refer at length to the events in which I have recently played a part, nor to the circumstances which have brought that event about. ... I can never forget your persistence in the course decided on. Let us but pursue it, and we shall yet arrive at the end of the goal. Our sacrifices are nothing compared with the objects in view.—Ever yours faithfully,

Thos. J. Kelly.

It would seem that Deasy boarded a ship at Liverpool disguised as a foreman while Kelly, sheltered by an old Irishwoman living close to the Fenian Arch, was later concealed at the house of Dr. Kelly, a dentist, in Oxford Road, Manchester. The house was raided several times by the police, but Kelly was either spirited away or hidden in the water cistern on the roof of the house. It is said that he spent some time in the Cheetham Hill area, where on one occasion he escaped from the police by changing clothes with a Father Tracey, before being taken to Liverpool by a Fenian who drove for a wine and spirit merchant. Concealed among the cases of wine he was delivered into friendly hands who assisted him to board a ship bound for America. It is strange to think that this man of action and adventure died in 1907 in America, where he worked as a Customs official of the New York Custom House, having himself been smuggled to America in a cabin specially constructed by a ship's joiner foreman called Eagan. One story is that Kelly having himself posed as a ship's porter carrying Deasy's baggage and pretending to haggle over a shilling tip, attracted so much attention that an unwitting policeman helped the "gentleman" on his way, admonishing the "porter" for his impudence.

Meanwhile the Irish quarters of Manchester were raided and searched and dozens of suspects, selected almost at random, were brought before the Magistrates. The *Manchester Examiner* reported that "In their zeal to capture all suspected persons the Manchester police . . . summarily apprehended on suspicion a highly respectable young gentleman, a land surveyor resident in Stockport who bore a strong resemblance to Colonel Kelly." For this unfortunate coincidence he spent thirty-six hours in a police cell.

The police were naturally more than anxious to save face. In their zeal the innocent and the guilty were dragged off to the cells, where some of them were the victims of a certain amount of private vengeance on the part of their captors.

One such unfortunate innocent was a Royal Marine on leave, who happened to be in the vicinity of the rescue and whose only sin was that he shared the same nationality as the Fenians and carried the name Maguire. His arrest was to become an important element in the case.

On a lighter note, one man with a strong Irish brogue turned up at court a few days later and surrendered to the Magistrate "as the only means I have of saving myself from being arrested over and over again wherever I go, as a Fenian". An Irish accent was not exactly advantageous at that time. Indeed it became almost a badge of Fenianism, as the authorities tried to compensate for their negligence in allowing Kelly and Deasy to escape. The names of the first batch of twenty-two prisoners were listed by *The Times* when they came up for remand— some of them still under assumed names. Guarding the police station was a group drawn from the same cavalry regiment that had cut down men, women and children of their own nationality in the infamous Peterloo Massacre in 1819. Manchester still retains the memory of its own martyrs who were killed at the assembly at Peter's fields and with whom the "Manchester Martyrs" are frequently confused.

Inside the Court, the charges were read out. Charged with wilful murder and riot were William O'Meara Allen and Michael Larkin; charged with riot and murder were William Martin, clerk aged 35; and described as well-educated; William Gould (a pseudonym for O'Brien) described as a clerk, aged 30; Louis Moore, joiner, 26; Patrick Hogan, labourer, 26; John Carroll, labourer, 23; Charles Moorehouse, clerk, 22; John Gleeson, labourer, 42; Patrick Barragan, labourer, 49; Henry Wilson, clothes dealer, 28 (outside whose home Kelly and Deasy were first apprehended); Michael Joseph Boyland, schoolmaster, 37; William Wells, labourer, 29; Michael Corcoran, labourer, 29; Edward Shore, alias Short (who was in fact Condon), described as a traveller, 26; John Butler, weaver, 54; Patrick Clooney, scavenger, 69; Patrick Kelly, labourer, 35; Michael McGuire, clothes dealer, Smithfield Market, 32; Patrick Daley, tailor, 36; William Lutler, striker, 19; and James Woods, hackler, 22.

The social composition of those charged is a good indication of the wide appeal of the Irish National cause amongst expatriates living in metropolitan Britain. This was no small caucus of restless officers from the United States or of frustrated intellectuals unable to find acceptance because of their Irish origins. It reveals a wide spectrum from labourers to men of some education, willing to risk their liberty and lives in a cause which was openly revolutionary and akin to treason and, what is more, a cause that no longer affected them in a personal sense since they had left Ireland. The agrarian system or personal suffering were there-fore less important than a strong sense of national solidarity with their fellow countrymen captured by the police. However, looking through the list one is forced to the conclusion that the main appeal is to the working class and small tradesman, who would in any event form the overwhelming majority of dwellers in "Little Ireland".

The prisoners now kept at the Central Police Station were given no chance by the fifty soldiers of the 57th Foot, commanded by a Captain

Halstead, to repeat the daring escapes of so many Fenian prisoners. An escort of 8th Hussars accompanied them when they were taken the short distance of 200 yards to the Court.

The streets were thronged with passive onlookers as they made their way to the Court, while at the rear of the police station the military were drawn up, each man supplied with twenty rounds of ammunition. Then started an identification parade that would never be accepted by a court of law in Britain today. The prisoners were all lined up against a wall, along the main corridor. No non-suspects were introduced amongst them. The witnesses to give evidence at the trial were then led past them. Not a word was spoken until the witnesses made their identification known to the Sergeant in charge.

Meanwhile more arrests followed, and by 21st September fifty suspects were in custody while arrests were still continuing. One of those arrested was Condon's colleague Nugent. Ten prisoners were, however, discharged on that date for want of satisfactory identification. At the same time the police were still hunting for Kelly. The neighbourhood of Eccles was raided and searched in a vain attempt to find the two wanted men. The police in the Manchester area were armed with cutlasses and every police station was supplied with loaded revolvers. The precautions that should have been taken earlier were being taken too late.

When the prisoners came before the Magistrate, all except Allen and Larkin said that they had witnesses to prove they were elsewhere when the van was attacked; but all were remanded in custody. As the prisoners rose in a body to leave the Court, a murmur of sympathy came from the women's section of the Court creating a moment of tension as it mingled with audible hisses from the public gallery, particularly as young Allen was being removed by the Constable-in-Charge. In the eyes of the press and the public he was already regarded as a guilty man.

It was, however, at the Coroner's Inquest, that the public first heard what was going to be the prosecution case against the accused men, when P.C. George Shaw gave his evidence:

> "On Wednesday afternoon I was on the prison van going from Manchester to the city gaol along the Hyde Road. There were two of us sitting on the lefthand side of the driver, myself and Constable Yarwood. Just before we got to the railway arch on the Hyde Road, I saw a number of men standing about on the lefthand side of the road."

At this point the Coroner interceded strangely by asking:

"What is the name of the man who is supposed to have shot the deceased?"

"His name is Allen. I identified him in the police court yesterday," replied Shaw.

"Where did you first see him?"

"I saw him before the van was stopped. He was the first man I saw and he was standing on the footpath on the lefthand side of the road, under the arch. He had a revolver in his hand. The van got about a dozen or fourteen yards through the arch before it was stopped."

Shaw went on to say that he did not know Brett was in the van. He got off directly it was stopped and did not see Brett until he was lying on the floor. In reply to the Coroner he said that he did not see Brett fall out of the van, but from behind the van he saw him lying on the floor at the back of the van.

"At that time there were some men on top of the van trying to break into it, and there were others with revolvers standing between us and the van protecting the men who were breaking the van open."

"Did you see Allen with a revolver?"

"Yes, he was the man who shot Brett. I saw him stand near the step and fire into the van. He discharged his revolver more than once."

"Now I wish you to be particular about this. Are you sure you saw him fire more than once?"

"Yes. He fired at me several times when the others were trying to get the prisoners out, and in firing at me he shot a man named Sprowson in the foot."

"Did you see him fire any shot at the door of the van which you suppose went through?"

"I saw him put his pistol to the door of the van, either at the key hole or the ventilator, a little above, but I think it was the keyhole, and I heard the shot fired. The moment the shot was fired someone called out from inside the van 'he's killed', the door was not open then. We were driven away from the van by the men who were guarding it with revolvers and directly after that I saw the van open and Brett lying on the floor. I do not know whether Brett ever moved or spoke afterwards but I should think he did not.

Some of the officers present helped him into a cab and he was taken to the infirmary."

Shaw then produced a policeman's hat with a bullet hole through the back. Cross-examined by the Jury Shaw referred to a woman's voice urging someone to shoot and, asked whether it was probable that Allen knew whether Brett was inside and whether this procedure was new, he said:

"Well, it is done sometimes in order that he may hear what is said. I think Allen must have known that Brett was inside because I heard someone call out 'he's inside the van'."

Apart from the fact that the police officer was hardly in a position to know whether Allen was aware of Brett's presence there was certainly no implication that he fired deliberately at Brett. Indeed, later at the trial Shaw agreed that the shot seemed to him to be at the lock. However, from the point of view of the law this was not strictly relevant, for as the Coroner was not slow to point out:

Whether the man knew that Brett was inside or not would not affect the legal aspect of the case hereafter. Any person firing a bullet into the van under the circumstances detailed would undoubtedly be deemed guilty of murder.

Examination before the Magistrates to establish a *prima facie* case against the accused started on Thursday, 27th September. The prisoners presented a formidable list and a formidable problem for the Court which would have to be satisfied that there was sufficient evidence against each individual to justify sending him for trial before a judge and jury.

Twenty-eight men faced the Court to hear the evidence against them. Allen, Shore (Condon) and Gould (O'Brien) were defended by Ernest Jones, barrister and champion of the working man. As a Chartist leader fighting alongside the redoubtable Feargus O'Connor, he himself had known the inside of an English gaol for two years and was a symbol of the common interest of radicals and Fenians which is examined in a later chapter. Unfortunately his disdain for the establishment almost immediately led him to clash with the Court and deprive the accused of a sturdy and able defender.

Michael Larkin along with five others was represented by Mr. Cottingham. Mr. W. P. Roberts was instructed by subscribers to a

defence fund and represented nine of the men; Thomas Maguire and
five others were defended by Mr. Bennett.

Almost immediately battle was joined by Ernest Jones over the handcuffing of the prisoners. "It appears to be discreditable to the admini-
stration of justice that men whom the law presumes to be innocent
until they are found to be guilty should be brought into Court handcuffed together like a couple of hounds." Mr. Jones supported by Mr.
Roberts and Mr. Cottingham asked that the handcuffs be ordered to be
taken off. The Magistrate, Mr. Fowler, insisted that the prisoners were
in the charge of the police authorities and that he had no power to
make such an order, but would only concede larger handcuffs if a
prisoner was suffering.

In spite of Mr. Jones' insistence that the Magistrate was the superior
authority in the Court and that there was adequate police protection,
Mr. Fowler refused to interfere.

Mr. Higgins, for the prosecution, outlined the circumstances of the
attack on the van. He admitted that there was doubt as to whether one
or more shots were fired but "it was certain that one shot was fired by
the man Allen through the ventilator. It was fired with deliberate aim,
and it took effect in the head of Brett, entering the skull on the right-
hand side and coming out on the other." But the real outcome was
never in doubt, for as Mr. Higgins pointed out: "If a number of men
associated themselves together for the purpose of making an attack
upon the police officer when that officer was in the execution of his
duty, according to the law of the country it was not only wilful murder
in the man who fired the shot but it was wilful murder in the case of the
others who were there, and taking part in that transaction, and assisting
in that unlawful act."

Constable Shaw testified that he saw Allen put his pistol to the keyhole of the ventilator and fire once, and that in the affray not less than
one hundred shots were fired; he had Allen impressed on his memory
from the first because of his daring behaviour. After the evidence of
Yarwood and Shaw and a short adjournment, Mr. Jones repeated his
application for the handcuffs to be taken off. He objected also to the
presence of part of a military force on the bench with the Magistrate.
Mr. Cottingham insisted that the Magistrate had power and authority
"to direct that the prisoners may be relieved from the pressure of these
manacles". Mr. Fowler remained adamant, whereupon Mr. Jones
astounded court and spectators alike by a daring, courageous and
dramatic exit from the Court.

Then as a member of the English Bar I decline to sit in any Court where the police override the Magistrate. I will not lend myself to any such violation of the ordinary course of justice. There is your brief, Mr. Roberts, I am sorry to return it but I cannot disgrace the Bar by proceeding with the defence.

Handing over his brief and gathering up his papers and umbrella, Mr. Jones marched dramatically out of Court to the accompaniment of loud hisses from the public gallery.

The demonstration had some effect, since ultimately the Magistrate retired to consult with Captain Palin as to the necessity of the prisoners remaining manacled. After twenty minutes he returned only to announce that it would not be prudent to remove the handcuffs. His reply was greeted with applause from the public gallery. As the proceedings continued, Mr. Roberts exploded in anger with words comparing the events to those which are now remembered as the trial of the Tolpuddle Martyrs. "Recollect we are in Manchester, we are not in Dorsetshire," he said. But Manchester was shortly to have its Martyrs too. The dispute continued angrily, Condon and another defendant refusing to be represented by any other than Ernest Jones.

Perhaps the most vivid picture was painted by one of the female prisoners in the van:

I was in the police van on the 18th of this month. I was in the alley. There were five more besides myself. Sgt. Brett was there. I remember the van being stopped. I heard a sound like a large stone being thrown at the side of the van, and then a pistol fired, like as it were at the horse's head in front of the van. Then someone came to the back of the van, at the outside and the trap door was opened . . . someone came and began to knock at the back of the door. Brett looked through the ventilator and said "Oh my God, it's those Fenians!" The women began to scream, and said they should all be killed. The man outside then asked Brett to give him the keys. The trap was then shut, Brett was doing his best to keep it shut. When the man asked for the keys Brett said he would not give them up. I could not see who the man was. He asked for the keys again, and said that if he would give up the keys they would do him no harm, but let two men out of the van. Brett said "No, I will stick to my post to the last." Someone then got on top of the van, got a large stone, and beat a large hole in the van over where Brett stood. Two of the women seized hold of Brett and tried to

THE TRIAL AT MANCHESTER

THE PRISONERS LEAVE NEW BAILEY FOR THE ASSIZE COURT

THE EXECUTION

pull him out of the way of the stones falling upon him. The stone did not fall through. The women said to Brett as they were pulling him back, "you'll be killed". A stone was then forced into the trap and Brett could not close it again. A man then put a pistol through the trap. Brett was looking through the higher part of the ventilator. I was looking lower down, and saw the pistol and I pulled Brett away and I said "Oh Charlie, come away, look there." I took hold of his coat and tried to pull him away, as I did so his head came on a level with the trap, and the pistol was discharged.

Here was direct evidence from the person closest to Brett that the direction of the fatal shot could not have been deliberately aimed at him.

Brett fell into a stooping position against the door. I could see the man who fired the pistol. I have seen him since at the City gaol. The man with the light coat and blue necktie was the man who fired. Allen came to the door and asked for the keys, but we said we dare not give them to him. He threatened to blow our brains out if we did not give them up. A woman then got the keys out of Brett's pocket and handed them through the opening . . . the door of the van was then opened and the women came out, I among the number. Brett fell out.

The witness then said she could pick out two men in the crowd, she only heard three pistol shots and saw nothing more as she fled to the security of the City gaol where she had been originally sent for stealing.

Indeed, it was one of the features of the trial that so much of the evidence came from prisoners who had much to gain from their testimony at the trial. One of them, young Baxter, a juvenile being transported in the van, heard a voice ask for the keys and the same voice saying, "Where's Pat Kelly?" He saw a man with a bunch of keys walking along the passage. A voice from the opposite box said, "I'm here." He heard another shot and later found the bullet. Similar evidence was given by another juvenile. Then followed a long procession of witnesses to identify the men in the dock. One of them advanced his views on Fenianism, "I believe they are a lot who want to upset the country, and murder everyone they come near who resist them." This man identified Shore (Condon). Proceedings also followed against a further six men arrested after the others, while three accused, Nugent, Lynch and Moore, were released for lack of evidence.

D

It was clear from the evidence that in spite of the number of shots fired the fact that there was only one fatality was a clear indication that there was no intention to take life if this could be avoided, and Mr. Cottingham put this to the Magistrate. "It is idle to say that men armed with dangerous weapons, some thirty to forty revolvers, with five or seven chambers each, and all of them loaded, if they came together for the purpose of sacrificing human life that they would not have done so."

It was also argued that the rescue was not illegal as the prisoners were wrongly imprisoned. In the submission for the defence by Mr. Cottingham the real nature of the offence as political rather than criminal emerged for the first time for a fleeting moment.

"The rescue that was attempted was not a rescue of an ordinary criminal, but of two persons who were not convicted of any offence at all, and who were only accused of a political crime."

But what political crime was more heinous than that of Fenianism, the "lot who want to upset the country"? The only achievement of the day was the release of two prisoners because of unsatisfactory identification.

According to Condon's later account;

> During the preliminary examination or trial, which preceded that before the Special Commission, the prisoners were chained two and two together, Allen being fastened to O'Brien and Larkin to me, so that one could not leave the Court for the most necessary purpose without dragging the other along with him. During all this time Larkin constantly recurred to Bolger's cruelty in goading him to his fate, and causing him to leave his aged mother, his wife and children helpless and destitute. These were allowed to visit him during the daily recess and, as we were always, except at night, chained together, I was constantly forced to witness the agony of the helpless victim and his afflicted family during their interviews.

Certainly the unfortunate Larkin suffered greatly and was to suffer yet more, but it is a matter of conjecture as to whether Bolger's action was to blame. Clearly, Condon was ill disposed to Bolger throughout the account, and at no time during the subsequent trial or documents is there any evidence of Larkin seeking to place responsibility for his presence upon Bolger. After forty years' exile and the rivalries that inevitably occur in émigré politics one cannot rely implicitly on this aspect of Condon's account.

While Larkin and his fellow prisoners suffered, Sergeant Brett was buried in the presence of civic dignitaries and a vast number of on-lookers and mourners. His widow and three children were given a pension for life. The cheerful and popular Manchester bobby was now a national hero and cards bearing his name and deeds were distributed amongst the crowds. No one regretted his death more than the Fenians themselves, for it cast a shadow over a daring rescue which to many Englishmen was regarded as cold blooded murder. It inevitably estranged sections of public opinion already prone to anti-Irish prejudice.

Nevertheless, in Ireland itself, bonfires burned to celebrate the release of Kelly and Deasy, celebrations that were to turn to grief and mourning before long—for now the trial was to begin, and the English demanded revenge.

2

The Trial

As the trial opened on 28th October before Mr. Justice Blackburne and Mr. Justice Mellor, photographs of the accused men and Swinburne's poem of passionate appeal on their behalf competed with one another for the custom of those outside. Admission was severely restricted by ticket only to the front rows and official portions of the Court, while the ladies' gallery was kept entirely clear. Twenty-six accused appeared in Court initially. The procedure of charging the Grand Jury whose decision to bring in a "true bill" was the prerequisite to a trial for felony has long since been abandoned in this country. Strange as it may seem today, another rule of procedure precluded prisoners from giving evidence themselves and it was still a novelty for witnesses to be called in their defence.

The trial in this case was held by a "Special Commission" and prosecuted by the Attorney General, evidence of the extreme seriousness with which the Government regarded the incident and the Fenian Movement which instigated it.

In this situation, before evidence had been given, the issue was virtually prejudged, particularly in view of the evidence given at the committal proceedings before the Magistrate, and by reason of the address to the Grand Jury giving the alleged account of the offences. Mr. Justice Blackburne described to the Grand Jury how Brett refused to give the keys up and "in consequence of his refusal he met his death by a shot in the head". He went on to say:

> The evidence goes to show that Allen was the person who fired the shot.

In the course of the first day the Grand Jury returned "true bills" against all the prisoners for murder, felony and misdemeanour and the five "principal offenders" were joined in one indictment. They were Allen, Larkin, Gould (O'Brien), Shore (Condon) and the curious outsider, the Marine called Maguire.

On the second day, the stage was set for the trial of the five men. As the judges took their seats at five past nine the crowd outside the Court was kept back by a wooden barrier specially erected outside the building. A military force of nearly 2,000 men assisted a large body of armed police in guarding the route and approaches from the gaol to the Assize Court, and escorting the van containing the prisoners. This time there was to be no possibility of a repeat performance of the rescue.

Two days earlier the *Freeman's Journal* reported that Mr. O'Donoghue, Member of Parliament for Tralee, had pressed the Home Secretary for postponement of the Special Commission which was to try the prisoners as they had not had time to prepare their defence—this was to no avail. Whilst most of the English press, and in particular *The Times*, strongly supported an early trial, the radical *Reynolds News* (a weekly journal of Politics, History, Literature and General Intelligence) on 3rd November, 1867, in its editorial, was to describe the Manchester trial as a "deep and everlasting disgrace" to English government, a result of panic.

> Because in an isolated attempt at the rescue of two men suspected of Fenianism, a policeman happened to be killed, a violent trembling seized the governing classes, and a yell of vengeance issued from every organ of the aristocratic plunderers of the English working classes. Wholesale and indiscriminate arrests were made. Before a particle of evidence had been formally obtained against the prisoners, their guilt was assumed, and their execution demanded. The crapulous and bloodthirsty old thunderer of Printing House-square declared that Mr. Allen must be hanged for the murder of Sergeant Brett. All the smaller fry of journalistic thugs took up the cry, each, according to his powers of utterance, yelling, or howling, or shrieking for the blood of these untried and simply suspected men.

Reynolds News attacked the Home Secretary for refusing Roberts' petition to postpone and/or move the trial to London;

> The world now sees that the aristocratic tiger has his old thirst for blood. Our Tory rulers still believe in terror, in torture, and in death. The rulers who have not the brains to devise beneficent reforms, have the heart to shed blood; the men who cannot comprehend how the affections of a warm-hearted race are to be gained by kindly treatment and equitable laws, have unbounded faith in the efficiency of hanging as a remedy for sedition. Yes, the

rulers of these realms place their reliance on the gallows; they cling to the hangman's rope as the cable of their salvation. The scaffold is their ark of safety, Calcraft is their saviour, and the strangling of political enemies their only means (as they fatuously imagine) of escape from the yawning hell of revolution.

Calcraft was the infamous but almost legendary hangman who prophetically was to be the triple executioner in November of that year.

On 12th October, *The Nation* (Dublin) had commented that there was "no hope of a fair trial for the prisoners given in the present state of the English people". A public effort was sponsored by the newspaper to collect money for the defence of those on trial. But the trial of Allen, Condon, Larkin, O'Brien and Maguire was to take its predictable course. The verdicts were a foregone conclusion. The Attorney General (Sir J. S. Karslake), Mr. Higgin and Mr. Hannen were Counsel for the Crown; Mr. Digby Seymour, Q.C., Mr. Sergeant O'Brien, Mr. Cottingham and Mr. Ernest Jones were to appear for the defence. Popular feeling ran high against the men in the dock and the Attorney General's closing speech for the prosecution was greeted with applause.

Leslie, in *The Irish Tangle*, wryly comments that: "Had they been Italian and used the same means to win a free Italy, they would have been deified in London as Garibaldi was. Irish Garibaldis were transported and hung." Indeed the nation that gave shelter to Kossuth and watched the struggles of Poles, Hungarians or Italians with sympathy had a blind spot where Ireland was concerned. It is perhaps difficult today—unless one looks at the situation in Ulster—to grasp the depth of anti-Irish feeling among many sections of English society from Queen Victoria down to penniless labourers or unemployed. Contempt, fear and hatred were emotions that guided the actions of governments and brutalised mobs alike. The attitude, while having a basis in the cry of "No Popery", was akin to racialism.

Not for nothing was Lord Salisbury at a meeting four years later to proclaim in all seriousness that "you would not confide free representative institutions to Hottentots for example", in a clear reference to Ireland. To his ilk, democratic institutions worked admirably when "confided to people who are of teutonic race". It was this sort of attitude with which men like Mr. Roberts and Mr. Digby Seymour had to contend. To make matters worse, the trial was held in an atmosphere of exaggerated fears and rumours, adverse comment in the press and public hostility in the locality.

Mr. Roberts, solicitor for the accused, was saved by the intervention of Mr. Digby Seymour from being committed for contempt of court by the presiding judge, Lord Blackburne, when he objected to all the jurors living in the neighbourhood of Manchester. Mr. Digby Seymour himself asked for the removal of the trial to the Central Criminal Court due to the "excited feeling which has not subsided since the lamentable occurrence".

The case was opened for the Prosecution by the Attorney General, who emphasised the legal rule under which several men could hang for the murder of one man by another—that when men combined together with a common design to rescue, were prepared to use violence if necessary, and death ensued, the crime was murder committed by all engaged in the rescue. In the Attorney's words, "all those who were aiding and assisting in enabling Allen to carry out the common object were equally guilty of the crime of wilful murder".

First to give evidence was Constable Yarwood, who testified that as the van was proceeding along Hyde Road, which was crossed by a railway arch, Larkin rushed towards the horses' heads, shot the horses in the neck and fired up at the officer in the box—although not taking deliberate aim. The Constable knocked Larkin's pistol up and it went off over his head. He then threw a stone which cut Larkin on the lip. Larkin fired and pursued him, and then fired a third shot.

He identified Allen and Gould (O'Brien) and said that he saw Thomas Maguire among the men in the embankment. The repeated identification of Maguire, who was later to produce a cast-iron alibi, is one of the curious features of the trial which casts grave doubts on evidence that on the surface sounds accurate and reliable. Yarwood had at the commital proceedings identified O'Brien as having shot the horse and he then referred to the presence of another man. This shadowy figure crops up on more than one occasion and remains one of the real mysteries for those examining the case dispassionately. Yarwood, curiously enough, saw no revolver in Allen's hand.

Constable Shaw then identified all the prisoners but, to be fair to him, expressed himself less than certain about Maguire, saying that he thought Maguire was there helping to break the van but that he did not get a clear look at him. Condon subsequently confirmed in his later account what should have been apparent to the Court, that Maguire was in no way connected with the rescue operation. Nevertheless, Shaw's willingness to testify even in this limited way against Maguire and the fact that he was vague in the extreme casts doubts on his certainty on the one crucial question—his identification of Allen. He repeated the evidence he had given before the Magistrate. He testified to seeing Larkin and Shore (Condon) throwing stones, but again could not swear to seeing revolvers in the hands of Gould and Shore, that is, Condon and O'Brien.

His evidence above all points to the real reason for the firing of the fatal shot. History should never be allowed to forget that it was Police Constable Shaw, not a witness for the defence, who said: *"My impression was that Allen fired to break the lock of the van."* Whatever view the reader may take about Allen's culpability, with which we will deal later, the motive was clear and logical.

Then came Thomas Patterson, a puddler, who showed his unreliability by telling the Court that he identified Maguire as having thrown up stones to Allen who went up to the door and placed his revolver to the ventilator.

George Pickup, a brickmaker, took the stand and told the Court he had seen Larkin hammering at the door with a hammer and "saw another man" fire at the door. He did not refer to Allen except that he recalled him saying to Kelly—swearing emphatically to this part of his evidence—"Kelly, didn't I tell you I would die and lose the last drop of blood for you?"

A hairdresser, John Griffiths, gave evidence that he saw Allen point his pistol "as I thought at the lock of the van", but he also identified Maguire as being among the men who were attacking the van. He recalled that Maguire had on an old fashioned hat, taller than those now worn. Maguire was also identified by a youngster of twelve, George Mulholland, who told the Court that he saw Maguire get on the roof and break it open with a big stone. He was not able, however, to say whether Allen or Larkin fired at the horses, although before the Magistrates he had sworn that it was Allen. His testimony seems somewhat suspect in view of the way it fitted in with previous evidence in spite of the initial contradiction before the lower Court. The last witness to testify on the second day, a railway clerk called John Bech, again identified Maguire as throwing stones.

When the proceedings opened on the third day the first witness was John Knowles, a grocer. He, too, testified to having seen Allen fire through the door of the van, but said that a man who got on top of the van was not one of the prisoners. Again, William Hughes saw Maguire handing up stones but stated that "*I saw a man hammering at the ventilator, and then he fired at it, that man was not one of the prisoners either*".

Edward Ridgway admitted that one of the prisoners not in the dock (Ryan) reminded him forcibly of the man who fired the shot at the back of the van.

In addition to these two references to another man, Frances Armstrong was to refer to "one man who came to the ventilator" who "had a slight moustache and another with a dark coat on". Allen was clean shaven and wore a light coat.

On Thursday, 24th September, *The Times* had described in its columns a suspect "of rather special importance" who was not apprehended. It went on:

> He is a man stoutly built, over the middle height, who took a leading part in attacking the rear of the van while others were assaulting it in front. Some bystanders saw him present a revolver at Police Constable Knox and Constable Connoll, those being the two policemen stationed on the footboard behind the van. He was also heard to say, "turn up the keys and let the prisoners out". The constables making no answer to the demand he and another fired at them, but neither of the shots took effect.

Certainly no such evidence on this score was adduced at the trial, and the "other man" remained shrouded in mystery. It is, however, to this day popularly accepted by most Irishmen familiar with the event that Allen did not fire the fatal shot. The historian cannot look the witnesses in the eye and cross-examine them. Only print remains to give their testimony, which undoubtedly weighs heavily against Allen. But O'Hegarty in his *History of Ireland Under The Union*, describing the trial as a farce, attributed the plan to Ricard O'Sullivan Burke and names the man called Peter Rice as having fired the fatal shot. This may well be based on Devoy's view. He writes:

> Then they found that O'Meagher Condon, who had been ordered to bring a sledge-hammer, a crowbar, and a set of burglar tools with which to open the prison van, had failed to bring them, and while they were trying to batter in the door with stones and pieces of timber, one man, Peter Rice, thought he would shoot out the lock and he fired a shot through the keyhole. The policeman (Brett) inside the van had, at the time, his eye to the keyhole unfortunately, and the bullet killed him.

The same view is accepted by Jules Abels who states that a sledge-hammer and crowbar had inadvertently been left behind. His version may well be based on the earlier account, but both conflict with Condon's denial and are obviously based on Bolger's report.

As to Allen, the evidence in his favour may at first seem unconvincing, but the correspondent of the *Cork Herald*, in a letter dated 13th November, 1867, reported the arrival in New York of seven of the men who attacked the van; one of the party admitted in his presence that he was the one who had fired the shot which killed Brett. He spoke with a Lancashire accent and gave no name. This would add substance to Condon's and subsequent versions.

What adds significance to this is that in giving his evidence Hughes described the other man who had fired as being five foot seven or eight in height wearing an overcoat with a velvet collar. Was he perhaps also the man described by Frances Armstrong or the man referred to in *The Times*, or was he Peter Rice or the man in New York? Or were all these four the same man?

The fact remains that three witnesses at the trial made specific references to someone other than Allen as having been closely involved in the shooting incident. Hughes and Ridgway actually went so far as to refer to another man as having fired into the back of the van.

Add to this the alleged admission to the American correspondent of the *Cork Herald* and the notice in *The Times*, and the doubts begin to mount. It would seem from these points alone that someone else was at the back of the van who may well have fired the fatal shot, and all this goes to make Allen's persistent assertion of his innocence more convincing, even to the most sceptical reader. It must also be considered in the context of the subsequent breaking down of witnesses and the acquittals in the trials following Allen's, and the recognition of Maguire's innocence. In both cases, the same witnesses had given evidence, and Maguire had been convicted on the same indictment and the same evidence as that which sent Allen to the gallows.

But above all, Condon's subsequent reference to Rice forty years later, when there was nothing to hide, raises a strong possibility that the shadowy figure at the back of the van, mentioned in *The Times* notice and in New York a short time later, may well have been Peter Rice, and that Allen was after all not the man who killed Sergeant Brett.

On the other hand other witnesses had no doubt that Allen fired the shot, although Thomas Barlow, who saw Allen pursued, stated that "Allen fired his pistol in the brickfield [where he was caught] at the ground, so as not to hurt anyone".

Emma Halliday repeated the testimony given before the Magistrate, as did Joseph Partington who at 12 years of age had been sent to prison for taking a shilling, an interesting comment on the social background of the times.

Thomas Sperry, employed by the Midland Railway Company, described how Allen was caught, while a cab proprietor, Henry Wilson Slack, was yet another of the long procession of witnesses to identify Maguire as being on top of the van. The third day finished with less vital witnesses, although the injured policeman, Sgt. Bromley, identified O'Brien as having fired at Constable Trueman, grazing his back.

On the fourth day Detective John Taylor described how he had seen Allen with a pistol in each hand, making a rush across the archway at the people on the right hand side of the arch, before running away. Constable Trueman saw Allen, with one foot on the cab's step, fire through the ventilator, heard a woman's voice cry out "he's shot" and then saw Allen look through the ventilator.

The cross-examination of witnesses was itself a revelation of the prejudice among many of the witnesses, and only the most salient features of the trial have been quoted in this necessarily much abbreviated account.

As to the van itself, a gunmaker named Thomas Newton who had examined it gave evidence that a bullet had gone through the side and struck against the door of a cell. Another had pierced the Royal Arms and another just at the corner of the rim. There was another hole on the roof, but there were no marks in the door either inside or outside. Although the van was recently traced to premises near Barton Airport, Manchester, where it was said to have housed a brood of hens, it would seem that it has now perished and will yield up no secret in this regard.

At this stage, evidence was given of warrants against Kelly from Manchester and Deasy from Ireland, and the case for the Crown was concluded.

Mr. Seymour then submitted that if Kelly's and Deasy's detention was unlawful through excess of jurisdiction or other irregularity, such as want of a proper warrant, then he and his friends would have the right to do their utmost to escape and therefore if a death were accidentally to ensue the offence committed would not be a capital one. He argued from Hawkins' *Pleas of the Crown* that this would reduce the charge to manslaughter.

Mr. Justice Blackburne, however, after a long and involved exchange of argument, did not regard this as applying to strangers who were not in custody; and although there was a warrant from Ireland which was not backed at the time of arrest, he was of the opinion that the Magistrates were perfectly entitled to remand them.

We think as at present advised, that even supposing the custody was illegal and irregular and supposing those who had the parties in custody held them under such irregular and informal warrants that they would have had a perfect right to have been discharged before a judge and that there was no legal justification for detaining them in custody, nevertheless we think it would form no excuse whatsoever for those who deliberately and with design engaged in the attack upon them, using dangerous violence, and killed them, though it was for the purpose of aiding an escape from what on that supposition was illegal custody.

Witnesses were then called for the defendants. Mary Flannigan, governess, said that on 18th September, the day of the attack, she was taking a walk in the Hyde Road and was speaking to a person named Wilson when she saw Gould (O'Brien) talking to some friends at ten minutes to four opposite the gaol gates on Hyde Road. However, it turned out that Wilson himself had been charged and that Kelly and Deasy had been to his home, so that this evidence was of no assistance.

Isabella Fee, who kept a public house on Rochdale Road, and her son both confirmed that Shore (Condon) was in their house at a quarter to four on the day of the attack, which occurred three miles away at four o'clock.

Neither of these witnesses really covered O'Brien and Condon, but such was not the case in relation to Maguire.

First to the witness stand came Elizabeth Perkins of Preston Court, Salford, a widow and sister of Maguire: "On the 18th he did not get up until half-past three in the afternoon because he was not well. My sister was living with me. She leaves for work at 5.30 in the morning. My brother did not go out until near seven o'clock that evening. My house is about 2 miles from Hyde Road."

Mary Ingham, a next door neighbour, said: "I saw Maguire on that day. He spoke to me through his bedroom window and asked me if he could come with me to a party. That was at half-past three exactly."

Elizabeth Ingham, also from next door, saw him crossing the yard at 4 o'clock, and this was backed up by James Grant and Elizabeth Blackburn, none of whom had any connection with Fenianism and who had seen him at various times between 3.30 and five o'clock.

Indeed, until four days before Maguire had been returning from a voyage to China and Japan as a Marine. He had spent ten years at sea and as he put it before the Magistrates: "I never had no correspondence with no one and there was never one of my people connected with Fenianism. I never was near the place, nor would I know my way about Bellevue. I never was out in that direction in my life."

It was only after the conviction that Maguire would be able to testify under the remarkable rules that then operated: "The witnesses against me have sworn falsely, I was not there. It was the third time I had been on furlough since I was in the Royal Marines, I had been three years in India, China, and Japan. I was paid, and came to see my friends on furlough. Having been for years to sea, and not much in England, I thought I would enjoy myself when I came here." His senior officers also gave him a good character—but this was to come later, and the Jury did not have the benefit of hearing it until they had passed judgement on him.

They did, however, listen to the speeches for the defence, which underlined the atmosphere in which the case was heard.

Mr. Seymour charged the Jury to say "I will never surrender to personal fear or to popular prejudice the keys that control my conscience."

"A temple of justice surrounded and protected in all its approaches, in all its secret passages and in its public halls, by banners erected for the occasion, and by military, infantry and horse, was no usual event," he told them. "It was not usual to feel that every second man, as one traversed the spacious corridors was a policeman in uniform."

He was, however, quick to disassociate himself, as an Irishman, from any sympathy with Fenianism in terms which must have irritated four of the five men. Perhaps, however, this was the only way to break down the Jury's inevitable prejudice against his submissions.

"Of all the curses that ever fell upon unhappy Ireland, Fenianism was the blackest and the worst," said counsel for the defence. "Nevertheless," he continued, "Fenians were upon trial but British Justice was on trial."

Witnesses had spoken of 50 to 60 men: others of 20 to 30: some of a whole arsenal of revolvers—others to a dozen men around with revolvers: why were no revolvers produced? "If the Crown had called the man who drove the police van, would not the Jury have felt more satisfied?" There was a discrepancy over who fired at the horses. Shaw said Gould (O'Brien) used a stone—others that he used a pistol. James Taylor did not recognise any of the prisoners at the commencement of the fray. The woman Cooper thought the shot came from higher up and not from the ventilator at all. "Frances Armstrong—according to her evidence the man who fired the pistol could not be Allen, the man whom she saw had a moustache. Allen did not fire upon the pursuers. Ridgway had identified another man but not Allen, although he saw firing through the ventilator."

All this was put to the Jury by defence counsel to sow the seeds of doubt that would justify an acquittal, but so strong must have been his fear of prejudice that once again in his conclusion he turned again to the evils of Fenianism—"it was but of mere fungus growth combined of ignorant Irish discontent and Yankee rowdyism. . . . There was not a single politician in his native land who had not condemned it: there was not a band of commercial men and capitalists who were not frightened of it: there was not an altar throughout the country where it had not been cursed."

Mr. Sergeant O'Brien next addressed the Jury for the prisoners Larkin and Maguire, to be followed by the Attorney General who hoped the conviction of the five men would have the effect of showing those who were foolish enough to believe that they could upset the constitution of the country by means of this so-called Fenian conspiracy that they were very much mistaken. Prompt justice would deter others.

Summing up, Mr. Justice Blackburne emphasised that the use of dangerous violence in the rescue made the offence murder, and included those assisting in the violence of others.

Strongly leaning towards the prosecution, he hardly dealt with the case of Maguire except to point out that "Mulholland, who was a sharp lad, spoke positively to seeing Maguire at the attack on the van".

Ignoring Constable Shaw and the evidence from inside the van, he advised the Jury that "there was very strong evidence that the shot which killed Brett was not merely fired in such circumstances that it would be likely to kill him, but there was strong evidence that it was intended to kill Brett".

After a summing up which lasted two and a quarter hours the Jury retired at 6.15 p.m. on the fifth day. At 7.30 they returned to give their verdicts—Guilty in every case. The only punishment for murder was death by hanging.

On 13th November the proceedings of the Special Commission ended, having extended over sixteen days from 9 a.m. in the morning to 6 p.m. in the afternoon, and frequently much later. Of the twenty-six prisoners named in the calendar, twelve were convicted, the five for murder and seven for riot and assault. Eight were released without any indictment being pressed against them; one was acquitted of murder. Two prisoners who had been found not guilty of murder, upon evidence almost identical with that given in the first trial, were convicted of riot and assault by another Jury.

In his 1908 article, Condon commented cynically that: "It is assumed to be a maxim of English Law that if a man be acquitted of any charge he cannot be tried for it again, but this notwithstanding, the acquitted prisoners were brought up and tried for the same offence under merely different name which, however, involved a lesser degree of punishment."

One of these, William Murphy, who on his release from imprisonment swore that he had never taken part "but would have been glad to", had urged all the prisoners then awaiting trial to die like men rather than dogs by pleading guilty to save their necks. This incident is recalled by Condon, but his memory as to its timing is at fault since any plea in mitigation would precede passing of sentence—not follow it as would be the case if Condon's account were strictly accurate, although in substance it is borne out by the known facts.

William Hogan, who lived in Birmingham and was a Director and Manager of an Insurance Company, had helped Condon's men to obtain revolvers for the attack on the van. Daniel Darragh and others had brought the arms to Manchester, and both Hogan and Darragh were later tried for their part in the supplying of weapons. Hogan was acquitted; he had a copy of one of the revolvers made—the gunsmith who made the originals swore it was one of his and his evidence was nullified by this remarkable stratagem. Darragh, however, was convicted and died in Portland Prison on 28th June 1868. Hogan took the body of his friend to Ireland, where he now lies buried in the Ballycastle Catholic Cemetery among his kinsfolk.

One of the survivors was John Carroll, the labourer listed in the original charges, and Condon's account closed on a note of compassion for his one-time comrade in arms in Hyde Road, Manchester, now living in poor circumstances. The great are remembered but the humble are too easily forgotten in the pages of history. Without the John Carrolls there would have been no heroes nor, for that matter, would there be any martyrs. Condon wrote:

> When we were condemned to death, Digby Seymour, one of the counsel engaged to plead for us, went down to the basement where

the rest of our men were kept, waiting to be brought up when required. Seymour addressed the men, dwelling impressively on our fate, and assuring them that they also would certainly be doomed to death unless they pleaded guilty, in which case he promised to secure a milder punishment for them.

Without an instant's hesitation William Murphy, a splendid type of a stalwart Tipperaryman, sprang up, and asked his comrades not to disgrace themselves and their race by pleading guilty before an English Court. They responded unanimously that they would not, under any circumstances, plead guilty, and Seymour left them, deeply disappointed and indignant at the failure of his attempt to degrade their Irish manhood.

The seven men sentenced to penal servitude were—Murphy, Brennan, Moorehouse, Carroll, Featherstone, Skelly of Ballaghdereen, and Reddin of Dublin. Some months later William Darragh, whom I had sent to procure the arms in Birmingham, was arrested, and with another man was sentenced to death. Their punishment was, however, commuted to penal servitude for life, and they were finally sent to Portland, where I was incarcerated. In a short time Darragh sickened under the brutality to which he was subjected, and after having been refused medical assistance for a long time, finally dropped down helpless one day in the prison yard, and was carried to the infirmary. We were not allowed to speak in the prison, but information was brought me soon that he was dying, and for the first and only time I asked a favour from the prison authorities—that of being allowed to see him before his death. The request was refused by the Director, who, however, turned to the Governor, while I was present, and asked how Darragh was doing. The other official answered that he was progressing finely. Two days later he was dead. His body, although buried, was, after much effort on the part of some members of Parliament and other friends, finally allowed to be disinterred and brought home for burial to his native town—Ballycastle in Antrim —where a beautiful monument has been erected over his remains. John Carroll of Manchester is the only survivor, besides myself, of those who were sentenced for participation in the rescue, and he is in poor health and in very moderate circumstances.

3

Protest: Fenians and English Radicals

As soon as the verdict was given, the thirty to forty members of the
English press who were present at the trial put their heads together. It
was clear to them that Maguire's alibi was not merely credible but true.
In spite of the verdict, the representatives of the press were convinced of
Maguire's innocence and acting upon this conviction they drew up a
petition addressed to the Home Secretary:

> We, the undersigned members of the metropolitan and provincial
> Press, having had long experience in courts of justice, and full
> opportunity of observing the demeanour of prisoners and wit-
> nesses in cases of criminal procedure, beg humbly to submit that,
> having heard the evidence adduced before the Special Commis-
> sion, on the capital charge preferred against Thomas Maguire,
> private in the Royal Marines, we conscientiously believe that the
> said Thomas Maguire is innocent of the crime of which he has been
> convicted, and that his conviction has resulted from mistaken
> identity. We, therefore, pray that you will be pleased to advise her
> Majesty to grant her most gracious pardon to the said Thomas
> Maguire.

This posed a difficult problem for the authorities. So many witnesses
had sworn to seeing Maguire playing an active part in the smashing
of the van that to admit error in his case was to admit the possibility of
error in the cases of the other four men. A jury sworn to give a true
verdict according to the evidence had found Maguire guilty, while a
large number of trained pressmen with no axe to grind had been so
outraged that they took the unprecedented step of petitioning the
Home Secretary.

On 4th November, 1867, the *Freeman's Journal* carried an editorial
against the carrying out of the sentences, pointing out that no malice
was present as the men had no knowledge that Brett was in the van;
there was a suspicion that witnesses were kept back who might have

given different versions of the facts; there was no proof of "deadly intent".

> The essential ingredient in murder is the deadly intent, the presence of malice, the mortal grudge. It was not to be found in the case of those unfortunate men, though the law holds them responsible. Had they not been mixed up with Fenianism they would never be hanged for a crime into which accident so largely entered. But they are Fenians, and an example must be made. The time has passed for hanging on account of mere political offences. Every civilized state in the world punishes such offences, however heinous, with penalties short of death. But the Manchester prisoners were not political criminals. They were accused, tried, and convicted of murder. We know it, but we are not the less satisfied that at bottom the offence is political, for it is grounded on a political motive—the forcible release of two Fenian ringleaders. It is impossible to disassociate the motive and its consequences. The whole business was very sad and very foolish. It began in violence and ended in blood. Had not the public mind been so inflamed, and had not the excitement outside unconsciously influenced the jury, a recommendation to mercy would probably have accompanied the verdict, on the ground that there was no evidence of deliberate intent. Judge Mellor, in passing sentence, held out no expectation of mercy. The unhappy men themselves did not expect it. All received the sentence with an heroic determination to meet death, and some rejoiced in the sacrifice they were about to make for their country. There was nothing theatrical in their demeanour. They knew their fate, and they met it with composure. Their blood will not serve any useful end. As Fenians they will suffer, but the principle of Fenianism will outlive their execution. We trust the humanity and good sense of Englishmen will interpose and save the lives of these men. They are not to be classed with those deliberate assassins whose lives the laws of England and of all civilized states justly demand.

But the law was to take its course and the condemned men required the comfort of the clergy. At this time a Monsignor Gadd of Manchester was on a holiday visit to Limerick Junction when he received an urgent message from Manchester's Catholic Cathedral, "Come back at once, five Irishmen are under sentence of death in Salford gaol."

Let him take up the story as he told it a few years later to Mr. John O'Dea:

> When I got back to the Cathedral, I hastened to the prison to make the acquaintance of my boys. I began to organise a little retreat. The five prisoners were placed in five condemned cells—all adjoining—three on one side of the corridor and two on the other. I used to kneel on the stone floor of the corridor. I could distinctly hear the boys making the responses to the prayers from behind the heavy, cumbrous, nail-studded doors of their cells, just as they could hear me offering up the prayers. This we did daily. I never had more devotional penitents in my life than the condemned Irishmen of Salford gaol.
>
> One morning I missed one of them. He had been taken by the Governor to the press gate before I arrived, a free pardon put in his hands and told to go. This was Maguire.

And indeed, faced with the all-pervading doubt about Maguire and the spreading conviction as to his innocence, the Home Office on the 21st November announced that he had been given a "free pardon", the traditional if unsatisfactory method of acknowledging a miscarriage of justice in England. And so Monsignor Gadd was left with only four condemned men in his charge.

But if Maguire was innocent and pardoned, there was perhaps hope of magnanimity from British Justice, in respect of the other four men, found guilty upon the evidence of the same witnesses whose testimony had convicted the pardoned man.

The *Freeman's Journal* on 15th November, 1867, wrote its editorial on the acquittal of Maguire. It asked if it had not occurred to the Home Secretary "that the witnesses, who made such a palpable mistake in the case of Maguire, might not have made mistakes about the other four?" It was fair to say that evidence should not be relied upon in other cases when it broke down so completely with regard to Maguire. "The passions and emotions of the Jury were aroused at the first trial. The witnesses were not sifted until subsequent trials, when some completely broke down, resulting in the acquittal of the second batch of prisoners."

The prevailing view at the time was undoubtedly that after the pardon, and bearing in mind that the offence was fundamentally political, the executions would not take place. It was a fair assessment to say that "it was universally concluded that, notwithstanding the abandonment by the Crown of the verdict on which they had been sentenced, they, because of their admitted complicity in the rescue, would be held to imprisonment—probably penal servitude—for a term of years."[1]

The *Manchester Examiner*, for example, commented that "we do not for a moment imagine that the capital sentence will be carried out in either case, but we none the less wish that the verdict had commended itself on more satisfactory grounds to the confidence of the public".

It has commonly been assumed by many Irishmen that there was in England either a lust for blood and vengeance or complete indifference to the fate of those who remained under sentence of death. That the radical movement in Britain came to the aid of the prisoners and that considerable sympathy was expressed by the more politically conscious working-class organisations is a side of the episode which has often been sadly overlooked by many Irish Nationalist commentators. Nevertheless it is precisely this factor which gives a new dimension to the story of the Manchester Martyrs and has a particularly important place in any attempt to analyse the significance of this event in Anglo-Irish history. In many ways it provides a key to contemporary attitudes concerning current problems in both Anglo-Irish relations and the position of Ulster.

In fact, all over Britain, for varied motives, ranging from the humanitarian opposition to a public hanging for a political offence by the Manchester Radical John Bright to the calculatingly scientific analysis of Karl Marx, there was widespread opposition to the executions.

The Times which, as the mouthpiece of the establishment, called for firmness in exacting the ultimate penalty, and the depressed and deprived mobs which were always available to intimidate radical and advanced thinkers, reflected only part of the popular mood. Prejudice against Irishmen in 1867 might well be compared to prejudice in England a century later against coloured immigrants, although it was national and religious rather than racial in character, and there existed many pressures against it. Edward Thompson's description of their relationship prior to the Fenian period illustrates the positive side.

> . . . there were many reasons why English Radicalism or Chartism and Irish Nationalism, should make common cause, although the alliance was never free from tensions. Antagonism could scarcely take racialist forms in the Army, Navy, or in the northern mill-towns, in all of which the Irish fought or worked side-by-side with English fellow-victims. From the days of the United Irishmen—

[1] T. D., A. M. and D. B. Sullivan, *Speeches From The Dock*, p. 377.

and the time when the Irish with their shillelaghs had helped in the defence of Thomas Hardy's house—a conscious political alliance had been maintained. English reformers generally supported the cause of Catholic Emancipation; for years, Sir Francis Burdett was its foremost parliamentary champion, while Cobbett furthered the cause . . . London Irish formed an Association for Civil and political Liberty, which had Hunt's and Cobbett's support, which co-operated closely with advanced English Radicals, and which was one of the precusors of the National Union of the Working Classes (1830)—itself the forerunner of the Chartist Working Men's Association (1836). There is thus a clear consecutive alliance between Irish Nationalism and English Radicalism between 1790 and 1850, at times enlivened and confused by the fortunes of the O'Connor family.[1]

Indeed, Irish immigrants had made contribution to Britain's first significant political working-class organisation, the Chartist Movement. Names like Bronterre O'Brien, Feargus O'Connor and Daniel O'Connell are part of the history of the English working-class movement and the directness and rebel spirit of these Irishmen was personified in Fintan Lalor, whose remarkably advanced social ideas were to be accepted by Michael Davitt in later years with regard to agrarian reform. Lalor's activities in the St. Patrick's Club and Fenian Movement were one of the many strands that bound English radicalism and Irish Nationalism. By 1851 already there were more than a quarter of a million Irish in England. Their numbers in Lancashire were particularly high and already, by the mid-nineteenth century, they formed perhaps more than a tenth of the population of Manchester, with about 200,000 living in the Lancashire area. Lancashire and Manchester also had a special significance in middle-class circles as the home of the Manchester Free Trade School of thought, which largely represented the aspirations of the more enlightened and practical industrialists with much working-class backing. Today, John Bright's economic liberalism might place him almost alongside the economic theories of Mr. Enoch Powell. But in respect of immigration there could be no comparison, and Bright's economic attitudes were shaped by the needs of the growing industrial areas of his period. Thus, when Fenian prisoners were facing death it was primarily the middle-class radicals and the organised working men of the cities who pressed the Home Secretary

[1] E. P. Thompson, *The Making of the English Working Class*.

and petitioned the Queen for their reprieve. On 21st November John Bright wrote in his diary:

> Home Office talk with Mr. Hardy in favour of Fenian convicts at Manchester; without avail, I fear Tories know little mercy; terror is their only specific.

On the same day a large meeting of London working men resulted from the feeling against the executions. It was held at Clerkenwell Green to adopt a petition to the Queen for clemency, addressed to Sir John Cavell, master of the household. It read as follows:

> At a meeting of working men numbering from 20,000–25,000 held at Clerkenwell Green this evening a resolution was unanimously passed that as Mr. Hardy, the Home Secretary, had declined to receive a deputation appointed by a meeting of working men held at this place on Sunday morning for the purpose of presenting a memorial on behalf of the Fenian convicts at Manchester, the deputation should wait upon the Queen at Windsor Castle on Friday morning to ask that her Majesty would be graciously pleased to accept such a memorial herself. I am deputed therefore, to solicit that you will most kindly exert your influence that her Majesty may so far condescend as to see the deputation, to receive from them the memorial. They wish it to be distinctly understood that they do not wish to trespass on the privacy of their noble and well beloved Sovereign: but, as hardworking men they hope the Queen will so honour them. Towards their Majesty they have the most devoted affection and loyalty.
>
> *Signed:* W. Clegg

Strange as the words may have sounded to a Republican and a Fenian, they illustrate some of the gulf between the reforming nature of most of the working-class movement in England and the insurrectionary, violent and conspiratorial character of Fenianism, born of an entirely different social and economic environment.

To the "Ribbonmen", the "Moonlighters", the "Invincibles", the Fenians or even the I.R.A., prepared to assert Ireland's nationhood by all means, this may sound like the language of deference, and there may be a tendency to look upon these manifestations as the conscience of England's "white liberals". This is to misunderstand the difference in development of the two movements. It should not conceal the strength and depth of moral outrage and solidarity felt by this advanced section

of British working-class organisation. It was, of course, very much in
the tradition and spirit which shaped Britain's Labour, co-operative
and trade union movements in a unique fashion, devoted to gradualism
and reform, rather than revolution. The social and economic cleavages
in English society, with perhaps the one potential exception of 1926,
were never to produce the violent responses that have occurred and are
still occurring in Irish struggles linked so closely with national and
religious passions. Nevertheless, English rule in Ireland was lambasted
among Englishmen.

The Radical working-class newspaper *The Beehive* of 19th October,
1867, commented in its editorial on Fenianism that it was the offspring
of injustice and misrule. "There is, however, no doubt of one thing,
that the gross injustice inflicted on Ireland for so many years by the
British Government and Legislature, has created a deep-rooted hatred
of English rule in the hearts of all true Irishmen, and that the perpetrators and abettors of this unjust Irish policy are now reaping the fruits of
their bad legislation."

A meeting of the International Working Men's Association (now
famous as the organisation in which Karl Marx first put forward his
theories), reported in *The Times* of 21st November and the *Reynolds
News* of 24th November, throws some light upon this difficult relationship. Discussion was sparked off by a letter from the President, Mr.
Beccles, condemning Fenian tactics while supporting their objectives.
Mr. Lucraft, who thought no good would come of using physical
force, commented that he "thought it strange that the Irish of London
had not made common cause with the English and Scots in the reform
agitation". The point was taken up by Mr. Weston, who commented
that "centuries of oppression and the hatred engendered by it could not
be cured by the concessions of reform which the English demanded for
themselves". Perhaps this is the key to any lack of sympathy in methods
if not in aims which may have existed between the Radicals in England
and the Irish Republicans.

Religious prejudice and bigotry had their part to play in no little
measure, but none could accuse the Fenians of being an arm of the
Catholic Church in spite of the fact that the mass of Fenians were
Catholics and the mass of Irish Catholics in England sympathised with
Fenianism—for as *The Times* pointed out on 3rd December: "It is
gratifying to record the consistent firmness with which our Roman
Catholic clergymen at least have discounted all sympathy with
Fenianism."

While it is true that many of the hierarchy condemned Fenianism from the pulpit, there can be no doubt that there was a great deal of underlying sympathy by many parish priests and others. According to Sir Leslie Shane, "No one cursed the Fenians more heartily than Cardinal Cullen," and Cardinal Vaughan later severely forbade the commemoration of the Manchester Martyrs in a Catholic Church. The Most Reverend Dr. Moriarty is always remembered for his attack —not on the Manchester Martyrs but on the leadership of the Fenian movement. "One word about the prime movers of all this mischief. If we must condemn the foolish youths who have joined in this conspiracy, how much more must we not execrate the conduct of those designing villains who have been entrapping innocent youth and organising this work of crime. Thank God, they are not our people, or if they ever were they have lost the Irish character in the cities of America. But beyond them are criminals of far deeper guilt—the men who, while they send their dupes into danger, are fattening on the spoils in Paris and New York—the execrable swindlers who care not to endanger the necks of men who trust them, who care not how many are murdered by the rebel or hanged by the strong arm of the law, provided they can get a supply of dollars either for their pleasures or their wants. . . . I preached to you last Sunday the eternity of Hell's torments. Human reason is inclined to say: 'It is a hard word, and who can bear it?' But when we look down into the fathomless depths of this infamy, the heads of the Fenian conspiracy, we must acknowledge that eternity is not long enough nor Hell hot enough to punish such miscreants." But this was not the attitude of the majority of devout Catholics. It is probable that the anxiety of both the British establishment and the Vatican to avoid hostility often led the leadership of the Catholic Church to accept the reports they received from official sources in the British Government concerning its actions in Ireland. Similarly, in a later period, while Bishops worked against Parnell and Davitt, many a Catholic clergyman was to grace their platform and express sympathy for their cause. The Church was not immune from diversity and had a strong radical wing in spite of the view commonly held by outsiders that its structure made it monolithic.

Some more depressed sections of the English working class, in expressions of national pride equal only to their economic degradation, were violently hostile to the Irish immigrants, and the Murphy riots in Ashton-Under-Lyne and elsewhere late in 1867 were to show that a great deal of latent chauvinism and religious bigotry could be whipped up by irresponsible agitators or the English authorities for the purpose of curbing the "revolutionary" Irish; but they were only one side of the penny.

On the other hand, O'Connell had brought Ireland to general attention "because his voice boomed in defence of every liberal cause during the years of European reaction".[1] Jews or Negroes, Greek patriots or Roman Catholics were seen by him to be suffering from the same basic evil. There were perhaps too few Irish patriots able to read beyond the misery of their own people to the wider implications of their struggle for liberty. It was left for the great James Connolly to write that "just as '98 was an expression of the tendencies embodied in the first Revolution, as '48 throbbed in sympathy with the democratic and social upheavals on the continent of Europe and England, so Fenianism was a response throb in the Irish heart to those pulsations in the heart of the European working class which elsewhere produced the International Working Mens' Association . . . ".

Similarly, there were too few radicals and reformers in England able to project themselves into the problems of the nation that was subject to their own rulers; but there were links and there was a common cause and common action just as there was uneasiness, hesitation and tension.

This must be seen in its historical context of the end of the mid-Victorian era when Englishmen of all classes could consider themselves almost as a master race. To cite one example of this attitude of mind. Professor Asa Briggs in his *Victorian People* takes the 1851 preface to G. R. Porter's *Progress of the Nation* as catching the contemporary mood: "It must at all times be a matter of great interest and utility to ascertain the means by which any community has attained to eminence among nations. To enquire into the progress of circumstances which has given pre-eminence to one's own nation would almost seem to be a duty." Of course, the top nation at this period was England and the attitude of the English could be summed up in a delightful contemporary couplet:

> Pride in their port, defiance in their eye,
> We see the Lords of human kind go by.

To those who saw the world in this light, the sufferings of the Irish were of little concern. One only needs to look at the contemporary literature to see such attitudes reflected among the respectable and the articulate, by whom Fenianism like Socialism was regarded with utter

[1] *Ibid.*, p. 103.

astonishment and lack of comprehension. Perhaps the most remarkable social comment comes from a mundane and matter of fact *Handbook to Manchester* published in 1841—and the same attitudes were still current in the late 'sixties, revealing a deep social cleavage in the heart of Britain itself. If the following could be written by a Mancunian of Mancunians, how much greater was the gap between the English establishment and the ideology that permeated all classes in England, on the one hand, and Fenianism on the other? In this case the object of the writer's comment was another group of people who were to become significant if not large by 1867.

> The morals of the lower classes in Manchester have suffered considerable damage by the influence of Socialism. That diabolical system has spread itself widely here. Its advocates have erected a large building in which their disciples assemble, and in which are delivered lectures suited to the tastes of the sect. These are frequently given on Sunday evenings and are attended with music and other circumstances that tend to destroy, especially in the minds of young people, all respect for the sanctity of the Sabbath. The undisturbed promulgation of Socialism has given a sort of latitudinarianism to immorality.[1]

The same writer, in respect of the Chartist Movement, expresses unreserved and unembarrassed satisfaction at the imprisonment and transportation of Chartists.

In addition to these diabolical Socialists and Chartists and the radicals of the Manchester School, there was to develop another ideology under the leadership of an unknown bearded foreigner who spent a great deal of his time in the British Museum analysing nineteenth-century capitalism. It was Karl Marx, who founded the International Working Men's Association to which James Connolly was to refer half a century later.

In the International Working Men's Association there was by definition an internationalist outlook and a readiness to understand the violent methods of Fenianism which shocked many moderates and liberal sympathisers with the Irish cause within England. Those who share with the writer a revulsion from much of latter-day Marxist ideology and practice cannot but pay tribute to the principled stand taken by this small but dynamic group in its attitude to the Irish ques-

---

[1] Love, *Handbook to Manchester*, 1841.

tion generally and to the Manchester Martyrs and the Fenian Amnesty Movement in particular.

Mr. Herman Jung, Secretary for Switzerland, recognised the Irish problem in its complexity in a discussion of the I.W.M.A. reported in *The Times* of 21st November:

> I am no abettor of physical force movements but the Irish have no other means to make an impression . . . while they are denounced as murderers, Garibaldi is held up as a great patriot; and have no lives been sacrificed in Garibaldi's movement? [It was perhaps the authentic voice of radical opinion in England when he went on to say—]I may not agree with the particular way in which the Irish manifest their resistance but they deserve to be free.

The differences were of means, not ends, and the same thread goes through most of the dialogue between English and other radicals with the Irish Nationalist Movement right up to the battle of Bogside which was to bring out British troops and interfere with the holidays of Britain's Prime Minister in August, 1969.

At the same meeting of the I.W.M.A. Mr. Lessner pointed out the appalling population figures in relation to Ireland:

> In the course of twenty years the Irish population has dwindled down from eight to five and a half million, and this decline is in consequence of British rule.

Mr. Eugene Dupont, Secretary for France, described Fenianism as "the vindication by an oppressed people of its right to social and political existence . . .".

> . . . what is the use of talking of legal means to a people reduced to the lowest state of misery from century to century by English oppression—to people who emigrate by thousands to obtain bread.

At the famous meeting of the Working Men's Association Mr. Dupont had pointed out that "the English working class who blame the Fenians commit more than a fault . . . they have the same enemy to defeat—the territorial aristocracy and the capitalists".

This was basically the attitude of the early Marxists to the Irish Question. Marx, who drafted the memorandum to the Home Secretary, did not approve of Fenian tactics. Engels, whose wife was a Fenian who had played some part in sheltering those involved in the

Manchester affair, described their tactics as a "foolishness which is to be found in every conspiracy". Mr. Morgan commented that "Englishmen applauded insurrection abroad, but denounced it in Ireland. The Irish had every reason to have recourse to physical force. Were they [the English] treated in the same manner by a foreign power they would revolt sooner than the Irish."

> "The crime of starving the Irish," added Mr. John Weston, "was far greater than the accidental killing of one man in trying to rescue the Fenian prisoners."

To Marx, the overthrow of English domination of Ireland was seen as a prerequisite to the overthrow of English and then European capitalism. In his view the Fenian Movement could set off a chain-reaction leading to the destruction of the old order throughout Europe, ushering in the era of proletarian rule. It was not primarily out of humanitarian concern for Ireland and its sorrows that so much of his interest was centred upon Ireland. In contrast, Engels was in a more personal sense devoted to the elimination of oppression in Ireland. With an Irish wife, committed to Fenianism, his was a closer and more personal interest.

Marxist thought was conditioned largely by Marx's own remarkable analysis of the workings of the Mid-Victorian capitalist system. In this, economic causation and the factors of productive relationships played the dominant role. Consequently, although Marx was far from unaware of the important role of national pride and national resentment, it was the wider implication rather than the intrinsic virtue of the Irish cause that really concerned him. Indeed, it was the view of many members of the Second International that the national question should not concern the proletariat and, even more, that it was reactionary to demand freedom and independence for all oppressed nationalities, since only the international proletarian revolution would be a solution to such problems.

To the humanitarian liberal or to the Marxist, the national problem poses a dilemma and a paradox. Intent upon uniting mankind, he has to recognise the desire of peoples to have their specific identity. Nationalism and liberalism, once associated in the ferments of 1798, 1830, 1848, the *risorgimento* and the unification of Germany, lost their common identity when nationalism was to become rampant in the form of the Third Reich and Mussolini's Roman Empire. It is the failure to distinguish legitimate national and cultural heritages from exclusive and domineering chauvinism that lies at the root of a problem that troubles radicals to this day. Lenin challenged the view of the Second International, and his recognition of the right of Finland to secede from the former Tsarist Empire is a lesson that should not be lost on those considering the problems of small nations in many parts of the world. Interestingly, there was never any doubt in the minds of liberal and left-wing thinkers about Ireland's right to self-determination.

The aligned problem is that every national movement has its right and its left, its liberals and its conservatives. These social and philosophical differentiations rarely emerge until the achievement of nationhood. Within the seed of every national movement lies the growth of diverse factions faced with the social problems of nationhood. In Ireland, this was to be compounded—and confused—by Partition, which once again divided men on the national rather than the social questions of the day.

Certainly, a cursory examination of Fenianism would lead one to accept that it was a nationalist rather than a social movement. It is true that like many sections of the Republican Movement after it, little thought appeared to have been given to any social policy, but the conspiratorial nature of the organisation would inevitably make the diffusion of such policies a difficult problem. The organisation was originally based on circles divided into sections of officers and men. The centre (Colonel) was known as A; nine sub-centres known as B or Captains; nine C's or Sergeants and for every C nine D's or privates. In theory, therefore, Fenians would only know their immediate associates. In practice their contacts were wider, otherwise the movement could not have spread its tentacles so widely. Although the early Marxists would not know what kind of an Irish Republic was being fought for, Marx and Engels nevertheless were foremost, through the I.W.M.A., in demanding the repeal of the Union of Ireland with the rest of the United Kingdom. Marx suggested to Engels that while the I.W.M.A. could conduct agitation for the repeal, Engels, who was in close touch with leading Fenians, should urge a programme embodying self-government and independence, agrarian revolution and protective tariffs against English competition.

There are many historians who would share the view expressed by Strauss in his book *Irish Nationalism and British Democracy* that "there was nothing in the contents of the Fenians' programme to mark it out as the expression of a social movement. The special interests of the oppressed classes of Irish society were never mentioned in it. But the radicalism of the Fenians, although confined to the political sphere, cut them off from the respectable classes of Irish Society."

Strauss recognises the important fact that while there was an intellectual leadership, the Fenians were composed almost entirely of working men, and the movement was opposed by the establishment in Ireland itself.

Michael Davitt later came to the conclusion that one of the reasons for the failure of Fenianism was its very secrecy, which cut it off from large sections of the people. He felt that it had not concerned itself with the day-to-day struggle of the tenant farmers against their landlords' extortions, being dedicated to the more abstract national ideal. It was the ideas of men like Davitt and Fintan Lalor which were to move the Irish question into the sphere of agrarian reform of a revolutionary type, while the voice of the mighty but enigmatic Parnell was to thunder in the British Parliament itself and urge the use of boycotts and resistance to eviction in the economic battle fought around the farm-steads of Ireland.

This tendency to view Fenianism as a purely national movement is understandable among Englishmen or even members of the I.W.M.A. The class differentiation in England and the long history of social conflict and reform had led to a sophisticated and more socially conscious radical movement. Probably few Fenians would have a great deal in common with the I.W.M.A., obsessed as they were with the grinding poverty and national humiliation which had been their lot under the Union. Their orientation was towards their brothers in Britain and the United States rather than towards the continent of Europe.

If Ireland had been an independent nation the process of social differentiation, which was such a distinctive feature of this era, would have almost certainly led to an open struggle for political power between movements representative of the conflicting social interests, but in Colonial Ireland this issue was interwoven with the problem of national self-assertion against English rule. To the Fenians and their opponents alike, nationalism and hostility towards England was the acid test of political sincerity; social interests they regarded as secondary matters which were unimportant except in so far as they affected the main issue, the attitude of the group or individual in the anti-English struggle. They did not know and probably would not have cared to understand, that the attitude was in the last resort determined by social interests and reflexes, and their inability to grasp this intricate but decisive connection enveloped the Fenians in an ideological fog which most of them found quite impenetrable. Internal dissensions, quarrels, expulsions and the more or less permanent impotence of the movement as such were the inevitable consequences of their failure.[1]

Nevertheless, the concept of an Irish Republic was now firmly established through the activities of the Fenians. Its democratic ideals and the idea that the Irish people must save themselves preceded by half a century the concept of Sinn Fein. It established the need for force of arms to free Ireland. It rejected religious sectarianism and relied upon the support of wage-earners and, while it was not a class-conscious movement as such, it was, whatever its critics may say, unequivocally opposed to the agrarian position and landlordism. Perhaps most important of all was the example it set to British and other colonial territories all over the globe, which in great measure explains the special role that Ireland now plays within the United Nations Organisation.

Indeed, James Connolly was to write that "deliberately unscrupulous and superficial historians have concealed the fact that the Fenians, like the Young Irelanders and like the men of '98 before them, were intent upon freeing the people from economic slavery as well as the nation from political bondage".

There is evidence that O'Mahony, who had organised a whole Regiment of Fenians to fight for the Northern States—the 99th New York National Guard of which he was appointed Colonel—had close connections with the I.W.M.A. Luby had attacked the social order of his day in the *Irish People*. He stood for social democracy—"An Irish Republic in which the people of Ireland would own the wealth of Ireland and administer it for the benefit of the entire community, and not for the selfish interests of a section or class."

It is no mere coincidence that with the inception of Fenianism in Ireland a determined labour agitation which culminated in a militant movement amongst journeymen bakers against night labour and in favour of a reduction of working hours, also began. Great meetings were held all over the country in which the rights of labour were vehemently asserted and the tyranny of the Irish employers exposed and denounced. In Wexford, Kilkenny, Waterford and elsewhere,

[1] Strauss, *Irish Nationalism and British Democracy.*

night labour was abolished. The movement was considered so serious that a Parliamentary Committee was sent to investigate it.

The problem is made more complex by the changing vision of the Fenians themselves and the individual rivalries within the movement. Luby became increasingly conservative. Stephens remained a social revolutionary. The ideas of European secret societies made a deep impact upon him but his movement was specifically Irish; his socialism was instinctive but he himself denied it by the early seventies: "Fenianism was wholly and unequivocally democratic although the utopian or childish theories of continental socialists did not by any means form part and parcel of my programme."

Stephens was neither "a red wrapped in a green flag" nor was he what is today termed a "Green Tory". He was, like the Fenian Movement itself and the Land League to follow, a specifically Irish phenomenon inevitably influenced by the wider social context and the social ideas, current among revolutionaries in Europe from utopian to scientific, from democratic to nihilist. Although its coherence was based on devotion to Ireland, Fenianism could not but be concerned with the plight of the Irish poor and its membership confirms its attraction to the underprivileged section of the community.

Thus Fenianism, while inevitably stressing the national ideal, was also concerned, if not as the primary point in its programme, with the social evils which afflicted Ireland. It could not be otherwise with a movement which drew its strength precisely from the most exploited elements and the new sub-proletariat born of the mass exodus from Ireland's shores in earlier years. Pearse's great funeral oration on the death of O'Donovan Rossa, couched in language worthy of Shakespeare's great orators, reflects the two intertwined aspects that inspired Irish Nationalism from '98 onwards and not least in the Fenian period:

> The clear true eyes of this man almost alone in his day visioned Ireland as we today would surely have her, *not free merely but Gaelic, not Gaelic merely but free.*

Seamus O'Kelly has done a service to the understanding of the social nature of Fenianism in his short book of Fenian portraits, *The Bold Fenian Men*. It explains what most historians have failed to grasp, that Irish Nationalism was as much a response to social evils as to the new assertion of nationhood witnessed in central Europe, Germany, Italy and elsewhere.

John O'Mahony and James Stephens spent much of their French

exile in democratic and republican circles in Paris where they were undoubtedly influenced by the ideas of secret societies in continental Europe. That Devoy and Stephens were members of the International is revealed in a letter from Marx to Engels of 17th December, 1866, where Stephens is described as "the most doubtful of our acquisitions". The full background to this temporary alliance is described in Desmond Ryan's recent book *The Fenian Chief*. But Stephens never attempted to impose his personal views on the movement as a whole.

Nevertheless, many who are steeped in Irish history and who learned the fate of the Manchester Martyrs at their father's fireside or in the cradle may find it difficult to accept the connection between Marxism and national discontent, anarchism and other European movements like the Carbonari or followers of Blanqui. The subsequent history of national independence movements throughout Africa and Asia reveals the same sort of alliances, often transitory and with a settling of scores after national victory. But none can deny that sympathy for the Irish cause in England has come and still comes from the radical and the left in English politics.

Marx above all believed that the repeal of the Union was an essential part of the English workers' programme. "Every one of its movements in England," he wrote, "is crippled by the disunion with the Irish, who form a very important section of the working class in England,"[1] but he gradually saw the Fenians rather than the English workers as lighting the touchpaper that was to lead to the chain-reaction of proletarian revolutions. Engels and his wife, Lizzie Burns, with a more direct interest, played a shadowy part in the story of the Manchester Martyrs.[2]

Engels has described with some passion the condition of the Irish in England, and there is no doubt that in human terms he was personally touched far more deeply than Marx, for whom Ireland was more a means than an end in itself. But one feature of the Fenian Movement which must have appealed both to the non-conformist radicals and Protestant workingmen, as well as to the early Marxists, was the non-sectarian nature of Fenianism, another aspect of its ideology which is often overlooked in the tendency to associate everything Irish with Catholicism. Of course, the overwhelming majority of Fenians were devout Catholics. But one only has to take the example of James Connolly himself or of Latin-American left-wing movements to see that radical politics and attendance at Mass are far from irreconcilable.

---

[1] Letter to Dr. Kugelmann, 29th November, 1869.
[2] Ralph Fox, *Marxism and The Irish Question*.

So-called "Catholic Marxists" are an important political element in several European countries. Basque priests arrested and imprisoned by Franco, French worker-priests or the Catholic priests of Ireland who fought alongside their flock are not eccentric oddities but part of a continuing tradition. Arthur Griffith recalls in his *Resurrection of Hungary* how Father Ignatius Martinovics founded a secret society to free the Magyars—a parallel for Ireland. Thomas Packenham describes the heroic exploits of Father Murphy, leader of the Wexford rebellion, in his *Year of Liberty*. Similarly, the fact that a Parnell or a Tone could assume the leadership of a predominantly Catholic country shows the religious tolerance that has been part of the Irish Nationalist tradition in contradistinction to the deliberately fostered exclusiveness of the Orange Order. This factor would help overcome the natural divergence of views between Fenianism and the radical left.

The non-sectarian nature of the Fenian Movement is worth special comment since today the term "Fenian" is frequently used as a term of abuse by extremist Protestant Unionists in Ulster and tends to imply adherence to Catholicism. Fenianism did not die in 1867 and its tradition was accepted in spite of the growth of the Orange Movement in Ulster. Thus, as late as 1905, Bulmer Hobson, a Protestant Republican, was able to write optimistically in a letter to Joseph McGarrity: "There is undoubtedly a new Ulster springing up . . . the Independent Orangemen . . . have made long strides in the right direction. They see that the interests of Ireland and those of England are opposed to each other, that the interests of Irish Protestants and Irish Catholics are identical. They appeal to join hands across the Boyne."[1]

Unfortunately, the battle of the Boyne is still the emotional prop of the Orange Order and the hopes expressed were to be shattered with the Partition of Ireland. But they have the utmost significance in showing the continuing tradition from Tone and Parnell to men like Erskine Childers who fought for a United Ireland at the time of the Treaty.

This ideological link with socialism was synthesised in the works of James Connolly before his tragic execution after the Easter rising. Writing on *Labour, Nationality and Religion*, Connolly declared:

> Socialism is neither Protestant nor Catholic, Christian nor Freethinker, Buddhist, Mahometan nor Jew; it is only human. We of the Socialist Working Class realise that as we suffer together, we must work together. We reject the firebrand of capitalist warfare

[1] *Irish Times*, 8th April, 1909.

and offer you the olive leaf of brotherhood and justice to and for all.

If men like Bulmer Hobson or James Connolly were to underrate the strength of religious antagonisms in Ireland, they nevertheless embodied the same spirit as that of the Fenians and were their logical successors. For among all the historians who write of the so-called failure of the Fenian Movement and among its contemporaries in Britain who criticised its methods or the subsequent shortcomings highlighted by Davitt, there is a tendency to underestimate the continuity of its traditions.

Not only did they become part of the heritage of Irish Nationalism in the twentieth century, but men like Devoy[1]—who established the *Gaelic American* after his split with O'Mahony—were the link and the driving force that led to 1916. It was Devoy who built up "Clann na Gael" and was the leading veteran Fenian in the United States, having given his support to the "New Departure" of Davitt's Land League. The Fenian tradition was embodied in men like O'Sullivan Burke, still active in the days that led to the Easter rising. It was above all embodied in the spirit of O'Donovan Rossa at whose graveside Pearse was to speak those prophetic and emotive words that above all sum up this continuity and lend credence to the thesis that Fenianism and the Irish Republican Brotherhood handed down a continuing tradition from 1898 to the men who were to fight and many of them to die in Easter Week half a century later. The link is both philosophical and personal, and the young man whose graveside oration epitomises it was to give his own life as proof of this inspiration. He was to be proved posthumously correct when he asserted that "the seeds sown by the young men of '65 and '67 are coming to their miraculous ripening bloom today. . . . Life springs from death; and from the graves of patriot men and women spring living nations. The defenders of the realm have worked well in secret and in the open. They think that they have pacified Ireland. They think that they have purchased one half of us and intimidated the other half, have foreseen everything, that they have provided against everything; but the fools! the fools! the fools! They have left us our Fenian dead; and while Ireland holds these graves Ireland unfree shall never be at peace."

[1] Devoy is perhaps best remembered for another and more remarkably daring rescue of Fenian prisoners in Australia. The story of the "Catalpa" rescue was to make him famous and hated by the British. He lived to see the Republic and the internecine strife that was to be Ireland's lot in the twenties, dying in 1929.

4

Efforts for Reprieve

With the Fenians in gaol the Radicals were not inactive. There was, of course, undisguised sympathy in the I.W.M.A., and the standing committee led by Marx was instructed to draw up a memorial address to the Home Secretary on behalf of the prisoners. Marx himself was particularly concerned in case the brutalities of the English Government in Ireland should divide both the English and the American workers as well as creating mutual hostility between the English and Irish. But this protest at the impending executions by what was then a small extremist sect was not confined to Marx and Engels, as the Clerkenwell meeting had shown.

At a public meeting on 20th November, at Cambridge Hall, Newman Street, London, the Reverend M. Solly, organiser of the Working Men's Club and Institute Union, addressed a densely crowded meeting of working men. He stressed the political nature of the offence and the fact that far from seeking plunder or exacting revenge the Manchester prisoners had believed they were acting on behalf of their country. He laid great stress on the need for the Government to see as its duty not so much the punishment of a crime as the removal of its cause. The implications for Ireland were only too apparent.

Charles Bradlaugh, the implacable radical and atheist whose refusal to take the oath of allegiance was to precipitate a remarkable Parliamentary storm, made an appeal for mercy: "If the Government is strong let it pardon, if it is weak and cowardly let it hang the men who are condemned." Bradlaugh was later to advocate a Commission of Englishmen and Irishmen to look into the problems of Ireland with a view to legislation.

A hundred years later English Members of Parliament were to be making the same demand over discontent in Ulster's Six Counties. Like Bradlaugh's, their appeal went unheeded until it was too late. At Cambridge Hall a resolution was passed expressing sympathy with Ireland, while at Manchester itself a crowded meeting in the Corn Exchange petitioned unanimously for the commutation of the sentences upon all the condemned men. The Reverend W. M. Call presided and two of the defence counsel, Messrs. Ernest Jones and Cottingham, addressed the meeting.

Meanwhile, in Birmingham disturbances took place on 20th November. There was scant support in this area for members of the Reform League who tried to elicit sympathy, and a rival mob of several hundred held a meeting in favour of hanging the Manchester convicts. Even *The Times* disowned this group, describing them in scathing terms. "They were," it wrote, "of a class who are always ready for any kind of mischief or depredations." Only a great force of well-armed Irishmen prevented the mob from sacking the Roman Catholic Cathedral.

Similarly, the deputation to deliver the Clerkenwell memorandum was followed by a hostile crowd groaning and hissing "with such vigour that the demonstrations must have attracted the notice of Her Majesty herself". This rival faction was, however, led mainly by subordinate members and officers of the Royal Household itself. Now, just as the Irish had joined in the defence of Thomas Hardy's house against such a mob, Englishmen were defending the liberty of Ireland and the lives of Irishmen against the same mindless hatred and violence. If Lord Salisbury could compare Irishmen with Hottentots and the Queen of England could look upon them as a "shocking abominable people—not like any other civilised nation", it was not surprising that this outlook was reflected at the other end of the spectrum of Mid-Victorian English Society, "The Lords of Human Kind" could be a pretty unpleasant lot, whether in the Palace or the streets of Birmingham.

Meanwhile, John Stuart Mill was to add his illustrious name to those who interceded for the condemned men, personifying the tradition of individual freedom and conscience which is one of the positive legacies of this period.

A somewhat isolated but remarkably eminent group of intellectuals including Frederick Harrison and Professor Beesly of *Punch* supported Mill and Bright, as did Odger of the Reform League. Their role is sometimes underestimated by those who, like Dr. Norman McCord, regard the extravagant demands for vengeance by *The Times* and the establishment or the pre-Powellite reaction of the Birmingham middle class as the true repository of English sentiment. History has always thrown up such antitheses, but it remains for the historian to account for the remarkable outcry against the hangings in the heart of the world's largest-ever empire, at a time when hanging for crimes much less heinous than shooting policemen was common practice, and public executions were an accepted part of the life of society. The Fenian amnesty movement, even after the Clerkenwell explosion had alienated moderate sentiment, deserves special attention. And it would be foolish for any historian to deny that in an era before mass communications, the greatest part of the population, as indeed today, tended to be apathetic and remote from these events. What is important and belittled by Dr. McCord and most nationalist historians, is the constant current of awareness that Ireland's ills were a function of English rule, and did not spring from original Irish sin. They asked essentially the question posed by Sydney Smith as long ago as 1807, quoted by Davitt in his *Fall of Feudalism in Ireland*. His words might be used in the House of Commons 152 years later in debating the "Ulster Defence Regiment".

> Before you refer to the turbulence of the Irish, to incurable defects in their character, tell me if you have treated them as friends and as equals. Have you protected their commerce? Have you respected their religion? Have you been as anxious for their freedom as your own? . . . You have confiscated the territorial surface of the country twice over; you have massacred and exported her inhabitants; you have deprived four-fifths of them of every civil privilege; you have made her commerce and manufactures slavishly subordinate to your own. . . . Nightly visits, Protestant inspectors, licences to possess a pistol, the guarding yourselves from universal disaffection by a police, a confidence in the cunning of Bow Street, when you might rest your security upon the eternal basis of the best feelings; this is the meanness and madness to which nations are reduced when they lose sight of the first elements of justice, without which a country can be no more secure than it can be healthy without air.

While these men of intellect were trying to stir a nation's conscience, power was still concentrated in the hands of a tightly-knit establishment, to whom the ills of Ireland or indeed of Manchester's mill-workers were of little direct concern, save for an incomprehension at their lack of gratitude.

At another level, action was taken by eminent counsel. William Digby Seymour, Michael O'Brien, Ernest Jones, James Cottingham

and Lewis L. Cane were reported in *The Times* of 21st November to
have submitted a long and complex legal memorandum for early con-
sideration by the Court for Crown Cases Reserved. It was sent to the
Trial Judges and was based on the allegation made at the trial that the
wrongful detention of Kelly and Deasy altered the nature of their
rescue. Lords Justices Blackburne and Mellor rejected it and declined to
put it before the other judges.

That night a member of the House of Commons, Mr. Maguire,
initiated a debate on the adjournment of the House, a weapon to allow
for immediate debate of urgent matters of definite and public importance. "Of the five men who were tried and sentenced to death at
Manchester," said Mr. Maguire, "not only had one received a free
pardon, but he had been restored to Her Majesty's service. The others
were to stand upon the scaffold, and the rope might have been fastened
round their necks by the evidence of several of the very people who
swore against the man just taken back into the Queen's service without
a stain upon his character. Five men were tried, convicted and sentenced
to death. Five others were tried, but the evidence on that trial was so
muddled and damaged that the prisoners were acquitted. Another
batch of prisoners were then arraigned for the same offence; but the
legal representatives of the Crown found that the evidence had been so
discredited on the trial of the second batch that they would not
proceed."

He asked for adjudication of the legal position by all the judges of
England not merely the Trial Judges, and moved the adjournment of
the House asking "in the name of all that was just . . . not to perpetrate
a legal murder".

Sir Patrick O'Brien, following, supported the contention that the
Trial Judges should consult their brother judges upon the memorandum.

Mr. Fawcett, while condemning Fenianism, added that he had no
hesitation in saying that "if the four men who were now condemned to
death should be hanged in Manchester on Saturday morning, that
event would send a thrill of horror into the hearts of thousands in this
country. Let us on this occasion exercise mercy, and while firm in our
policy let us be determined to do all we can to ameliorate some of the
wrongs under which Ireland suffers."

Sir George Bowyer observed that the United Kingdom was the
only country in the civilised world where the right of appeal in criminal
cases did not exist. He asked the Government to suspend the sentences

until the point of law was argued out. (While it was possible to appeal at this period, an appeal was only possible if the Trial Judge gave his consent.)

Mr. Serjeant Gaselee, Sir Colman O'Loghlen, Mr. Bagwell and Mr. Rearden joined in asking for a postponement.

Mr. Gathorne Hardy, the Home Secretary, backed up the two Judges and thought it illegal for him to interfere with the decision. However, Mr. Montague Chambers pointed out that to advise Her Majesty to exercise her prerogative could not be an illegal act. Replying, Mr. Gladstone observed that when the Trial Judges reserved a point for the Court alone, their judgement was final and the Attorney General asked the House to accept their judgement as final. Mr. Chamber's point went unanswered. The ageing Prime Minister, Lord Derby, was not willing to advise a reprieve for the condemned men. All the agitation on their behalf appeared to have failed.

However, on the same day Mr. Carey, replying in the House of Commons to a question from Mr. Watkin, told the House that the reprieved Maguire had been "restored to the service". Indeed, Maguire returned whence he had come to the Marines, but it was only a few months before he was discharged on the pretext of redundancy when there was a cut in personnel. The movement for mercy had grown and reached the seat of Government. Here was a ray of hope which, only three days before the day fixed for the executions, was strengthened tenfold when on 22nd November *The Times* was able to announce the commutation of O'Meagher Condon's sentence:

> We have very great pleasure in announcing that upon the recommendation of Her Ministers, Her Majesty has been graciously pleased to respite the capital sentence upon the convict Shore, in whose favour it may be remembered that he was unarmed when apprehended and that he was not proved to have been armed during the fatal affray.

This provided an excellent but hardly plausible pretext for what was a far more compelling reason, namely Condon's—or Shore's—American citizenship and the fear of antagonising American sentiment. In his 1903 account of the end of the trial Condon himself stressed the role of the United States Government:

> Even the London *Times*, whose prominent characteristic is not that of praising Irish Revolutionists, frankly admitted that "on the

part of all four there was not a symptom of flinching". In that paper, I may add, it was remarked that I "spoke with a decided American accent", while others declared that, by my utterances in the dock, I deprived myself of whatever chance of life I might have had before. I was respited on the day before that fixed for the execution on the imperative demand of the United States Government, cabled by Secretary Seward a second time, and my sentence was finally commuted to penal servitude for life. At the end of eleven years, however, and on the reiterated demand of our Government, backed by twice-repeated joint resolutions of Congress, the last of which followed the presentation on my behalf of the most numerously signed memorial ever presented to that body, I was released, but was not allowed my liberty until placed on a steamship bound for New York, and I was moreover prohibited from entering the British Dominions for at least twenty years.

But how pleased was *The Times*? It was *The Times* which in its editorial on 4th November had written:

The result of the first trial under the special commission at Manchester has more than justified the refusal of the Home Secretary to admit the plea for delay. The sentence pronounced not only records the righteous doom of our law upon a conviction for murder, but will be sanctioned by the reason and conscience of the whole community.

We cannot entertain any doubt that both Shore and Maguire wilfully aided and abetted in Brett's murder.

It would be an act of criminal weakness to spare the lives of men who have shed innocent blood in the prosecution of an enterprise which aggravates the guilt of murder itself.

Ironically, Maguire was now back with the Marines helping the nation that was to take the lives of his compatriots. But *The Times* had not excluded Maguire from its call for retribution. Condon was now reprieved because of mitigating circumstances which were admitted by the Ministers of the Crown but had not been admitted by *The Times*.

The Times was not merely the voice of the establishment. It represented the general tenor of the Press with regard to the Manchester episode. The men of Clerkenwell were sneered at—the dictates of law and order were such that blood would have to be shed at Salford gaol.

But consciences were roused in many parts of the country by the question which Charles Bradlaugh had put at Clerkenwell:

> How could they take those lives with the consciousness that if we had governed Ireland better these things would not have happened?

In an editorial on the pardon of Shore the *Freeman's Journal* of 23rd November argued that there was more evidence to link him directly with the Fenian organisation than in respect of any of the others. Constructively Shore was just as guilty of murder as the others. American intervention prevented his hanging. Shore was as guilty or innocent of deliberate murder as the others:

> Some too sanguine friends of humanity believed a reprieve would be granted at the last moment. Late in the night they expected the telegraph would announce the joyful tidings, but none came. A blood-offering was necessary, and a terrible example must be made! We are sorry the powerful London press did not exert its influence for mercy. Had it done so England would have been spared the calamity of today. It is the act of the country, not of the Government, which would only be happy to be relieved from responsibility if the nation interposed. There has been a dogged determination from the beginning to shed blood, in the hope of extinguishing Fenianism by terror of the gibbet. We fear the example will produce the contrary effect.

Sympathy was expressed in various ways—from the old lady who turned up at Salford gaol with a pint of beer—"a little luxury" for Allen—to the Dowager Marchioness of Queensberry who wrote to the condemned men enclosing £100 for Larkin's family. When Larkin read this letter he was overcome with tears. John Bright's Diary records: "The Marchioness of Queensberry's letter to them is beautiful; my eyes filled with tears as I read it."

> My dear friends, [she wrote] It may be that these few lines may minister some consolation to you on your approaching departure from this world. I send you by the hands of a faithful messenger some help for your wife, or wives, and children, in their approaching irreparable loss, and with the assurance that so long as I live they shall be cared for to the utmost of my power. Mr. MacDonnell, the bearer of this for me, will bring me their address, and the address of the priest who attends you.

It will also be a comfort for your precious souls to know that we remember you here at the altar of God, where the daily remembrance of that all-glorious sacrifice on Calvary, for you all, is not neglected. We have daily Mass for you here; and if it be so that it please the good God to permit you thus to be called to Himself on Saturday morning, the precious body and blood of Our Lord and Saviour and our Friend will be presented for you before God, at eight o'clock, on that day—that blood so precious, that cleanses from all sin.

May your last words and thoughts be Jesus. Rest on Him, Who is faithful, and willing and all-powerful to save. Rest on Him, and on His sacrifice on that Cross for you, instead of you, and hear Him say: "Today thou shalt be with Me in Paradise." Yet we will remember your souls constantly at the altar of God, after your departure, as well as those whom you leave in life.

Farewell! and may Jesus Christ, the Saviour of sinners, save us all, and give you His last blessing upon earth, and an eternal continuance of it in heaven.   CAROLINE QUEENSBERRY.

Hope remained to the very end, encouraged by the news of Maguire and Condon. Father Gadd expressed this feeling in his reminiscences:

Two days before the date appointed for the execution, Edward O'Meagher Condon—an American subject—received his reprieve. (It was not however till eleven years later that he was set at liberty on condition of his being banished for twenty years.) Then we began to think that, after all, the dread penalty of the law would not be carried out to its fullest extreme. There was hope and a strong one, that the remaining prisoners if not pardoned at any rate would receive a reprieve.[1]

Meanwhile, after the failure of the petition, preparations were made by Mr. Finlan of the Clerkenwell protesters to demonstrate by a funeral march. Some objected, as it would bring them into conflict with the authorities.

As the last-minute attempts to secure a reprieve were rejected, and as the 22nd November, 1867, came to its close and the harrowing farewell of Larkin to his family had passed, the three men drew up their final declaration for posterity:

[1] O'Dea, *Story of the Old Faith in Manchester.*

DECLARATION OF WILLIAM PHILIP ALLEN

I wish to say a few words relative to the charge for which I am to die. In a few hours more I will be going before my God. I state in the presence of that great God that I am not the man who shot Sergeant Brett. If that man's wife is alive, never let her think that I am the person who deprived her of her husband; and if his family is alive, let them never think I am the man who deprived them of their father.

I confess I have committed other sins against my God, and I hope He will accept of my death as a homage and adoration which I owe His Divine Majesty, and in atonement for my past transgressions against Him. There is not much use in dwelling on this subject; by this time, I am sure, it is plain to see that I am not the man that took away the life of Sergeant Brett.

I state this to put juries on their guard for the future, and to have them inquire into the character of witnesses before they take away the lives of innocent men. But, then, I ought not to complain. Was not Our Saviour sold for money, and His life sworn away by false witnesses? With the help of the great God, I am only dying to a world of sorrow to rise to a world of joy. Before the judgement seat of God no false witnesses will be tolerated; everyone must render an account for himself.

In reference to the attack on the van, I confess I aided in the rescue of the gallant Colonel Kelly and Captain Deasy. It is well known to the whole world what my poor country has to suffer, and how her sons are exiles the world over; then, tell me where is the Irishman who could look on unmoved, and see his countrymen taken prisoners, and treated like murderers and robbers in British dungeons?

I forgive all the enemies I ever may have had in this world. May God forgive them. Forgive them, sweet Jesus, forgive them! I also ask pardon of all whom I may have injured in any way.

May the Lord have mercy on our souls, and deliver Ireland from her sufferings. God save Ireland!

William Philip Allen.

DECLARATION OF MICHAEL LARKIN

Men of the World,—I, as a dying man, going before my God solemnly declare I have never fired a shot in all my life, much less the day the attack was made on the van, nor did I ever put a hand to the van. The world will remember the widow's son whose life was sworn away, by which he leaves a wife, and four children to mourn his loss. I am not dying for shooting Brett, but for mentioning Colonel Kelly's and Deasy's names in court. I am dying a patriot for my God and my country, and Larkin will be remembered in the time to come by the sons and daughters of Erin.

Farewell, dear Ireland, for I must leave you, and die a martyr for your sake. Farewell, dear mother, wife and children, for I must leave you all for poor Ireland's sake. Farewell, uncles, aunts and cousins, likewise sons and daughters of Erin. I hope in Heaven we may meet another day. God be with you. Father in Heaven, forgive those that have sworn my life away. I forgive them and the world. God bless Ireland!

Michael Larkin.

DECLARATION OF MICHAEL O'BRIEN

I have only to make these few remarks; I did not use a revolver or any other firearm, or throw stones, on the day that Colonel Kelly and Captain Deasy were so gallantly rescued. I was not present, either, when the van was attacked. I say this, not by way of reproach, or to give annoyance to any person; but I say it in the hope that witnesses may be more particular in identification and that juries may look more closely in the character of witnesses, and to their evidence, before they convict a person to send him before his God.

I trust that those who swore to seeing me with a revolver, or throwing stones, were nothing more than mistaken. I forgive them from my heart, and likewise I forgive all who have ever done me or intended to do me any injury. I know I have been guilty of many sins against my God: in satisfaction for those sins I have tried to do what little penance I could, and, having received the Sacraments of the Church, I have humbly begged that He would accept my sufferings and death, to be united to the sufferings and death of His innocent Son, through Whom my sufferings can be rendered acceptable.

My Redeemer died a more shameful death, as far as man could make it, that I might receive pardon from Him and enjoy His glory in Heaven. God grant it may be so. I earnestly beg my countrymen in America to heal their differences, to unite in God's name for the sake of Ireland and liberty. I cannot see any reason, even the slightest, why John Savage should not have the entire confidence of all his countrymen. With reference to Colonel Kelly, I believe him to be a good, honourable man, unselfish, and entirely devoted to the cause of Irish freedom.

Michael O'Brien.

5

The Scaffold High

The last public execution in England took place outside Newgate prison, London, on 26th May, 1869, when Michael Barrett was hanged for his part in a Fenian bomb explosion near Clerkenwell prison, but the execution of Allen, Larkin and O'Brien was "an event which, of its kind, has excited more public interest than any execution within the memory of living man".[1] But in spite of the daring of the crime, the national attention focused on the trial and the macabre spectacle so well prepared and dramatically staged, *The Times* was able to report that "there have been very few executions in a populous city at which there have been so few general spectators".

Probably not more than 2,000 saw the hanging and among the 8,000 to 10,000 present there was no demonstration of feeling for or against. In contrast to the previous night and early morning there was a "decorous silence" induced by the horror of the occasion. The crowd which had gathered around the well-guarded scaffold melted away as the night wore on and only the 2,000 "specials" filled the space in front of the drop and the prison wall.

As the day dawned a slight November mist began to thicken into a yellow murky fog and the number of spectators swelled rapidly. Like a huge fortress, the dim outlines of the massive prison loomed through the gloomy fog with an air of unreality. Inside the prison a couple of children played on the judges' benches of the sessions house, oblivious to the drama being enacted outside, and their laughter was the only sound which broke the stillness of the silent interior.

On Friday night the condemned men had bid farewell to their relatives. Only Allen was refused the consolation of seeing the girl he loved, and after writing letters and drawing up their declarations they spent their last evening in prayers and meditation. Only the raucous noises of the crowd outside disturbed their religious observances, in which they were comforted by three Catholic clergymen, Father Gadd,

[1] *Annual Register*, 1809, p. 59.

the Very Reverend Canon Cantwell and the Reverend Father Quick.

A double flight of steep wooden stairs of about 35–40 steps awaited their last journey to the hangman's noose. Still nervous to the end, the authorities placed stout ladders against the towers on the prison walls, so that in the event of an attack the troops could easily reach the platform and defend the building.

When the condemned men were awakened at their own request at five o'clock, the gallows outside were shrouded in darkness. After Mass, the prisoners partook of Holy Communion and each man in turn denied having shot Brett. Until the last they wanted to make a final statement from the scaffold, but they were induced to forego this final demonstration by the priests. As the crowd outside riveted their eyes on the scarcely perceptible gibbets the three men remained in prayer until their last breakfast at 7 a.m.

At about a quarter to eight the hangman, Calcraft, and his assistant entered the cells and each of the prisoners was pinioned in his own cell. They were bound with strong leather straps passing round the waist and smaller thongs binding their elbows to the back, and others fastening down the wrists in front of the stomach. They remained unflinching throughout, and their priests stood beside them exhorting them to courage and firmness, which they displayed throughout their ordeal. Pinioned as they were, only able to move their feet, later secured upon the scaffold, they "manifested a remarkable fortitude. Not one of them flinched in the least."[1] Not a word was said.

Meanwhile the tramp of soldiers was heard through the fog in the gaol yard, and a company of 720 Highlanders drew up with fixed bayonets beneath the scaffold on either side. Two smaller detachments of eighteen to twenty men ascended the platform built on a level with the scaffold. Simultaneously the heads of a line of soldiers arose above the parapet of the railway viaduct. By this time the fog was so dense that objects could only be faintly distinguished at a distance of thirty yards. For a few fleeting moments, absolute silence prevailed.

Then, just after eight, came the ritual processions as the human sacrifices were led to the scaffold. First came the Reverend Canon Cantwell repeating the litany of the Catholic Church. By his side was Allen, desperately concealing any outward appearance of weakness, ghastly pale, uttering the response "Lord have mercy on us" in a firm voice. "As he ascended the staircase he seemed to summon all his courage, and he succeeded so far as to be able to confront the crowd with an

---

[1] *Ibid*, p. 160.

unshrinking countenance." "O'Brien," reported *The Times*, "stout and powerfully built, looked perfectly resigned, anxiously and fervently looking at the crucifix, repeating in firm accents 'Christ hear us, Christ graciously hear us'." By contrast, the small undersized figure of Larkin needed support as he also prayed on his way to the scaffold, but as he neared the head of the stairs he gave one hasty glance at the black beams overhead and seemed to stumble or faint.

Only a partition separated the victims from the platform outside, and at about five minutes past eight the door was flung open and Allen, clasping his crucifix, appeared. As this happened almost every head in the crowd was uncovered. Immediately the executioner, Calcraft, assisted by one Armstrong, placed the noose around Allen's neck and pulled a thin white cap over his ashen face before stooping to tie his feet together. Through all this Allen continued in fervent prayer.

Then followed O'Brien, with remarkable courage. "On his fine manly face the closest scrutiny could not detect a trace of weakness."[1] He turned to Allen, shook his head, and kissed his right cheek through the thin white cap, speaking a final word that will never be known. Then he himself was capped, his feet bound and he was placed alongside Allen on the drop.

Last came Larkin, who was led directly to O'Brien's left. He seemed to stumble and regain himself and after the white cap was placed over his head he fell against O'Brien who turned to him firmly and spoke a few words of encouragement. For a moment the hangman disappeared from view and, as the three men stood before the crowd, their words "Lord Jesus, have mercy on us" rang out. Suddenly the bolt was drawn by the hangman and the men dropped. A subdued hum of terror and surprise ran through the crowd.

Almost at that very moment a loud explosion shook the air and the riflemen stood ready to use their arms, but it was only a fog warning on the nearby railway. The rear portion of the crowd rushed back upon the barriers and a series of rushes followed that could well have resulted in serious injury to the spectators. The obscene spectacle was over for them, but there remained a postscript. The *Annual Chronicle* for 1867 reported that "Allen was dead in about a minute; but the death of his fellow criminals was more painful, both Larkin and Gould (O'Brien) appearing, from the vibration of the ropes, to struggle. Gould was next to yield, and about two minutes later the stillness of the rope showed that Larkin had ceased to live."

[1] T. D., A. M. and D. B. Sullivan, *Speeches From the Dock*, p. 397.

G

According to *The Times*, however, Allen died instantly as did
O'Brien, but "Larkin's suffering was very great and it was nearly two
minutes before he ceased beating the air in ineffectual struggle". *The
Times* blamed this on "clumsy adjustment of the rope".

But the gruesome truth was not disclosed until some years later,
when Father Gadd told the full story of those last terrible minutes in an
account reported by John O'Dea.[1]

> Young Allen died instantaneously. His neck was broken. The other
> two ropes, stretched taut and tense by their breathing twitching
> burdens, were in ominous and distracting movement. The hangs-
> man had bungled! For Larkin and O'Brien the drop was too short.
> Canon Cantwell and Father Quick had retired as soon as the
> bodies fell. So had the Governor and the other prison officials.
> None remained but Father Gadd, old warder Kirtland and the
> hangsman. Calcraft then descended into the pit and there finished
> what he could not accomplish from above. *He killed Larkin.*
>
> Then he turned his attention towards O'Brien, but O'Brien was
> in the Monsignor's charge and he forbade the hangsman to touch
> him. Poor O'Brien's hands were clasped within the Monsignor's
> own. His fingers touched the crucifix the chaplain held. For three-
> quarters of an hour he breathed and for three-quarters of an hour
> the good priest knelt, holding the dying man's hands within his
> own, reciting the prayers for the dying. Then the long drawn out
> agony ended.
>
> O'Brien the last of the three was dead. After a while the bodies
> were cut down and Father Gadd saw them buried in quicklime
> within the unhallowed precincts of the city.

In his *Reminiscences of Manchester*, published in 1905, Mr. Louis M.
Hayes recalled the hangings, which he always associated with Bridge
Street, now a thriving area of offices and shops:

> Owing to the crowds which it was anticipated would attempt to
> witness the execution, some of the streets leading to the Prison
> were intersected with powerful barricades to prevent accidents.
> Amongst those so protected was Bridge Street, and it was a dismal
> experience to walk down this street as I did, on the afternoon
> before the morning of the execution, and see these melancholy
> preparations, and the wooden scaffolds built out from the wall of

[1] O'Dea, *Story of the Old Faith in Manchester.*

the prison. How human beings could gather as they used to do in vast crowds to witness the sufferings and death of their fellow-creatures is to me a strange mystery. When I again passed those prison walls after all was over, all trace of what had taken place had, as far as possible, been removed. The bricks had been replaced, leaving, however, black patches of mortar, which stood out distinctly from the old, and whenever from time to time I passed the prison in after days, I could never help feeling, as I looked at those black patches in the wall, that they were associated with the death-struggles of those unfortunate young men.

Let us be thankful that public executions are now things of the past, and that people are precluded from witnessing such demoralising exhibitions. The wonder is that they were ever permitted by law, or that it could be imagined that the actual sight of such scenes could do anything but harm to those who gathered at them.

In what he described as a "dull and uninteresting" street neither the black patches nor the prison remain to recall this tragic and obscene spectacle. But it took much campaigning to end public executions, which were supposed to exercise a deterrent effect. That the last public execution in Britain was also of a Fenian prisoner is perhaps symbolic of the interaction of brutality in an oppressed nation with brutality in the oppressor. That it did not deter but provoked the opposite response, whether in public or behind prison walls, was to be proved by the execution of the leaders of the Easter Rising which awakened a nation from its slumbers and provided the Martyrs whom Ireland all too often needed to inspire its will to free itself from outside rule.

6

The Boys Who Smashed the Van

William Philip Allen, with his pale face, high cheekbones and flowing hair, had taken a leading part in the assault upon the van. Dedicated to the Fenian cause—some would say fanatically—he was quite prepared to lay down his life for its leaders. Indeed there was almost a premonition of this when he spoke to Kelly on his release: "I told you, Kelly, I would die for you before I parted with you"—or words variously reported to that effect. It was Allen whose spirited and reckless disregard for his own safety along with his colleagues made the rescue possible, and it was he who took personal responsibility for seeing that Kelly was safe before his own capture, in the course of which he was severely beaten by the mob.

Witness after witness testified that Allen appeared to lead the attack, and although he denied having fired the fatal shot there can be no doubt that this young man was a natural leader. How much his other talents might have contributed to the Fenian Movement we shall never know, but as so often is the case in revolutionary action the lead in action is taken by those who have scarcely reached manhood.

The son of a Protestant father and a Catholic mother, he was born in Tipperary but moved at a very early age to Bandon, County Cork, where his father became Bridewell keeper. His religious background must have contributed to a breadth of understanding and experience, for at one and the same time he attended regularly both Catholic and Protestant schools in Tipperary. What must again be remembered is that one of the features of Irish history smothered by the divisive struggle between the Orange and the Green is that many of the great leaders in the struggle for national freedom from Wolfe Tone onwards have been Protestants and, particularly, dissenters.

But Allen himself, after attending a Catholic Mission in the town, was received into the Catholic Church by the local priest along with his sister, while his four brothers remained in the Protestant faith. Commenting on Allen and the other prisoners, Father Gadd later said, "I never had more devotional penitents in my life than the condemned Irishmen of Salford gaol."[1]

Like the great majority of Fenian supporters, he was a manual worker. The strength of the Fenian Movement "lay in the shop assistants, clerks and working men in the towns, and the agricultural labourers and small farmers in the country. The comfortable classes, the large farmers and the upper classes, were outside. But the mass of the people were with it."[2]

Apprenticed as a carpenter at Brandon, Allen found work in Cork for about six months before returning home. He then went to Manchester to join some relatives and was engaged to a girl in the city at the time of his execution. He spent a few weeks in Dublin as a builder's clerk and in the summer of 1867 he made his fateful return to Manchester. While in prison he was visited by his mother, two aunts and his fiancée, Mary Ann Hickey, who was heartbroken and desperate at the plight of young Allen.

All the indications are that he must have been one of Kelly's close associates in Dublin, and it is no accident that in his extremity Kelly turned for help to Allen and his friends after the arrest in Oak Street. In all probability the two had been in contact before that event, particularly as Condon and O'Brien would have provided another link with Kelly.

All eyes were upon Allen during the trial, and although the strain showed upon him, all accounts bear witness to the fact that he endured not only the physical pain of his capture and subsequent handcuffing with fortitude but he mastered his feelings to a degree that all but concealed his obvious sensitivity. The recklessness of his leadership on Hyde Road was matched by his remarkable self-control in the dock and upon the scaffold. Confronting the Court upon his sentence, his speech followed the best tradition of speeches from the dock, all too often the only platform open to those Irishmen who laid down their lives for national emancipation during the years of the Union.

My Lords and Gentlemen,—It is not my intention to occupy much of your time in answering your question. Your question is one that can be easily asked, but requires an answer which I am ignorant of. Abler and more eloquent men could not answer it. Where were the men who have stood in the dock—Burke, Emmet and others, who have stood in the dock in defence of their country? When the question was put, what was their answer?

[1] O'Dea, loc. cit. [2] P. S. O'Hogarty, *History of Ireland Under the Union.*

Their answer was null and void. Now, with your permission, I will review a portion of the evidence that has been brought against me.

Interrupted by Mr. Justice Blackburne, he was told that it was too late to criticise the evidence: "If you have any reason to give why, either upon technical or moral grounds, the sentence should not be passed upon you, we will hear it, but it is too late for you to review the evidence to show that it was wrong." Allen went on:

No man in this court regrets the death of Sergeant Brett more than I do, and I positively say, in the presence of the Almighty and ever-living God, that I am innocent, aye, as innocent as any man in this court. I don't say this for the sake of mercy: I want no mercy—I'll have no mercy. I'll die, as many thousands have died, for the sake of their beloved land, and in defence of it. I will die proudly and triumphantly in defence of republican principles and the liberty of an oppressed and enslaved people. Is it possible we are asked why sentence should not be passed upon us, on the evidence of prostitutes off the streets of Manchester, fellows out of work, convicted felons—aye, an Irishman sentenced to be hanged when an English dog would have got off. I say positively and defiantly, justice has not been done me since I was arrested. If justice had been done me, I would not have been handcuffed at the preliminary investigation in Bridge Street; and in this court justice has not been done me in any shape or form. I was brought up here, and all the prisoners by my side were allowed to wear overcoats, and I was told to take mine off. What is the principle of that? There was an obvious object in that; and so I say positively that justice has not been done me. As for the other prisoners, they can speak for themselves with regard to that matter.

And now with regard to the other means by which I have been identified. I have to say that my clothes were kept for four hours by the policemen in Fairfield Station, and shown to parties to identify me as being one of the perpetrators of this affair on Hyde Road. Also in Albert station a handkerchief was kept on my head the whole night, so that I could be identified the next morning in the corridor by the witnesses. I was ordered to leave on the handkerchief so that the witnesses could more plainly see I was one of the parties alleged to have committed the outrage. As for myself, I feel the righteousness of my every act with regard to what I have done in defence of my country. I have no fear. I am fearless of any punishment that can be inflicted on me. One remark more. I return Mr. Seymour and Mr. Jones my sincere and heartfelt thanks for their eloquent and able advocacy regarding my part in this affray. I wish also to return to Mr. Roberts the very same. My name, Sir, might be wished to be known. It is not William O'Meara Allen. My name is William Philip Allen. I was reared in Bandon, in the county of Cork, and from that place I take my name. I am proud of my country, and proud of my parentage. My Lords, I have done.

Forty years later Condon was to collect money for Allen's father, who was active in the Fenian organisation, although he took no part in the rescue.

The most impressive-looking of the men in the dock was Michael O'Brien, known to the world as Gould until he revealed his identity in his final speech to the Court. He also had close links with Kelly, having served as a Sergeant in the same Regiment during the American Civil War in the United States Army. He was known to the Fenian Movement as Captain O'Brien.

Tall, broadshouldered and resolute, his demeanour throughout his trial and on the scaffold did not belie his physical appearance. To the last affectionate embrace he seemed to encourage the other prisoners. Even the most hostile commentators at the time could not fail to pay tribute to his courage and bearing.

A County Cork man, he was born at Ballymacoda where his father rented a large house until, like many others, he was dispossessed in 1856 under the oppressive laws that forced so many Irishmen across the sea. Young Michael was apprenticed to a draper on Youghal, and it is perhaps significant that "in the absence of an industrial working class, shop assistants formed the most radical element in the town population and were therefore the most susceptible to the Fenian gospel of separation".[1]

O'Brien himself became an assistant in a leading drapery store in Cork before emigrating to the United States, where some of his relations had already transplanted their roots. Joining up at the outset of the Civil War, he won rapid promotion and it appears that he eventually rose to the rank of Lieutenant.

Returning to Cork at the end of the war, he again started work as a shop assistant. His disappearance the night before the Fenian rising leads

[1] Strauss, loc. cit., p. 148, et seq.

one to assume that he played some part in it. He was known to the authorities to have been in Dublin and Liverpool in the autumn of 1866, where he associated with other Fenians. At the previous Winter Assizes in Liverpool he was tried with two or three others on a charge of having in his possession a number of rifles belonging to the Government after the police had discovered a cache of arms in Liverpool, but was acquitted. It was as a result of this and a subsequent warning that the American Government refused to intercede on his behalf when he failed to follow their advice, and there was much criticism of the American authorities, particularly their representative, Adams. The Secretary to the U.S. legation, Moran, sternly informed O'Brien that he had received sufficient warning from the American Consul at Liverpool not to put himself in any danger again, and "Mr. Adams regrets to learn that you have failed to follow that prudent advice."

Having no relations and few close friends in Britain, O'Brien travelled frequently between England and Ireland on Fenian business and was believed from the information available to have been very active and energetic as a Fenian organiser.

By contrast, Larkin was an older man, small and slightly built. To *The Times* it seemed that "there can be little doubt that he was the victim of such men as O'Brien". The only married man of the five convicted, he had worked as an operative tailor for four years in Manchester and, as far as the authorities were concerned, he had not shown any Fenian tendencies until a year or two before the trial. However, he had then become an active Fenian and collected subscriptions from other supporters. Intelligent looking, with a small beard, small in stature, his was the hardest ordeal. As a family man he left a wife, Sarah, and four children, who saw him in his cell the night before his execution. From Lumagh in King's County, his grandfather had been flogged and transported in 1798 for his part in the rebellion when he refused to inform upon his comrades. His father had died only four months before the execution.

He worked for many years as a tradesman, having a good English education, and in 1858 left Parsonstown for England, where he married and worked hard to improve his business. A mild and inoffensive man with sober habits, he was caught up in the wave of national resentment at the appalling condition of his native land. Abandoning his personal security in his business and family life, he chose a path which led him to the scaffold. If he alone among the executed men displayed any sign of weakness, he had the most to lose and his, perhaps, was the greatest dedication and sacrifice. He was a sick man and had no personal motive or ambition in involving himself so actively in the destinies of his fellow Irishmen.

It is only when the Michael Larkins of this world have come forward that revolutionary movements attain any real significance. Speaking after Allen, he addressed the Court with great dignity and humility:

> I have only got a word or two to say concerning Sergeant Brett. As my friend here said, no one could regret the man's death as much as I do. With regard to the charge of pistols and revolvers, and my using them, I call my God as a witness that I used neither pistols, revolvers, not any instrument that day that would take the life of a child, let alone a man. Nor did I go there on purpose to take life away. Certainly, my lords, I do not want to deny that I did go to give aid and assistance to those two noble heroes that were confined in that van—Kelly and Deasy. I did go to do as much as lay in my power to extricate them from their confinement; but I did not go to take life, nor, my lord, did anyone else. It is a misfortune that life was taken; but if it was taken it was not done intentionally, and the man who has taken life, ye have not got. I was at the scene of action when there were over, I dare say, 150 people standing by. I thought, my lord, I had some respectable people to come up as witnesses against me. I am sorry to have to say, but as my friend said,—I will make no further remarks concerning that. All I have to say, my lords and gentlemen, is that so far as my trial went, and the way it was conducted, I believe I have got a fair trial. So far as my counsel went, they have done their utmost in the protection of my life; likewise, my worthy solicitor, Mr. Roberts. But I believe the old saying is a true one: what is decreed a man in the page of life he has to fulfil, either on the gallows, by drowning, death in bed, or on the battlefield. So I look to the mercy of God. May God forgive all who have sworn my life away. As I am a dying man, I forgive them from the bottom of my heart. May God forgive them.

Then came O'Brien's scathing indictment:

> I shall commence by saying that every witness who has sworn anything against me has sworn falsely. I have not had a stone in my possession since I was a boy. I had no pistol in my possession on the day when it is alleged this outrage was committed. You call it an

outrage; I don't. My name is Michael O'Brien. I was born in the County of Cork, and have the honour to be a fellow-parishioner of Peter O'Neill Crowley, who was fighting against the British troops at Mitchelstown last March, and who fell fighting against British tyranny in Ireland. I am a citizen of the United States of America, and if Charles Francis Adams had done his duty towards me, as he ought to do in this country, I would not be in this dock answering your questions now. Mr. Adams did not come, though I wrote to him. He did not come to see if I could not find evidence to disprove the charge, which I positively could, if he had taken the trouble of sending or coming to see what I could do. I hope the American people will notice that part of the business. The right of man is freedom. The great God has endowed him with affections that he may use, not smother them, and a world that may be enjoyed. Once a man is satisfied he is doing right, and attempts to do anything with that conviction, he must be willing to face all the consequences. Ireland, with its beautiful scenery, its delightful climate, its rich and productive lands, is capable of supporting more than treble its population in ease and comfort. Yet no man, except a paid official of the British Government, can say there is a shadow of liberty, that there is a spark of glad life amongst its plundered and persecuted inhabitants. It is to be hoped that its imbecile and tyrannical rulers will be for ever driven from its soil, amidst the execration of the world. How beautifully the aristocrats of England moralise on the despotism of the rulers of Italy and Dahomey;—in the case of Naples with what indignation did they speak of the ruin of families by the detention of its head or some loved member in a prison. Who have not heard their condemnations of the tyranny that would compel honourable and good men to spend their useful lives in hopeless banishment?

At this point the judge intervened to appeal to the prisoner for his own sake to cease his remarks. "The only possible effect of your observations must be to tell against you, with those who have to consider the sentence. I advise you to say nothing more of that sort. I do so entirely for your own sake."

Undaunted and defiant to the last, O'Brien continued:

They cannot find words to express their horror of the cruelties of the King of Dahomey because he sacrificed 2,000 human beings yearly, but why don't those persons who pretend such virtuous indignation at the misgovernment of other countries look at home, and see if greater crimes than those they charge against other Governments are not committed by themselves or by their sanction? Let them look at London, and see the thousands that want bread there, while those aristocrats are rioting in luxuries and crimes. Look to Ireland; see the hundreds of thousands of its people in misery and want. See the virtuous, beautiful, industrious women who only a few years ago—aye, and yet—are obliged to look at their children dying for want of food. Look at what is called the majesty of the law on one side, and the long deep misery of a noble people on the other. Which are the young men of Ireland to respect—the law that murders or banishes their people, or the means to resist relentless tyranny and end their miseries for ever under a home Government? I need not answer that question here, I trust the Irish people will answer it to their satisfaction soon. I am not astonished at my conviction. The Government of this country have the power of convicting any person. They appoint the judge; they choose the jury; and by means of what they call patronage (which is the means of corruption) they have the power of making the laws to suit their purposes. I am confident that my blood will rise a hundredfold against the tyrants who think proper to commit such an outrage. In the first place, I say I was identified improperly, by having chains on my hands and feet at the time of identification, and thus the witnesses who have sworn to my throwing stones and firing a pistol have sworn to what is false; for I was, as those ladies said, at the gaol gates. I thank my counsel for their able defence, and also Mr. Roberts, for his attention to my case.

O'Donovan Rossa was later to describe him as "one of the truest and one of the noblest; as devoted as a lover and as courageous as a lion".

The most brilliant oratory came from Edward O'Meagher Condon who, according to *The Times*, "excelled all the other convicts in his zeal for the Fenian cause".

He, too, had held a commission in the U.S. Army as a Captain in the Civil War. He was an Irish-American and his citizenship, added to the fact that he had not carried a revolver during the assault on the van, were the factors which allowed for his eventual reprieve. In his own account of the incidents published forty years later he claimed or

admitted responsibility for organising the attack on the van as leader of
the north-west section of the Fenian Movement.

> My Lords [he said], this has come upon me somewhat by surprise.
> It appeared to me rather strange that upon any amount of evidence,
> which, of course, was false, a man could have been convicted of
> wilfully murdering others he never saw or heard of before he was
> put in prison. I do not care to detain your lordships, but I cannot
> help remarking that Mr. Shaw, who has come now to gloat upon
> his victims, after having sworn away their lives,—that man has
> sworn what is altogether false; and there are contradictions in the
> depositions which have not been brought before your lordships'
> notice. I suppose the depositions being imperfect, there was no
> necessity for it. As to Mr. Batty, he swore at his first examination
> before the magistrates that a large stone fell on me, a stone which
> Mr. Roberts said at the time would have killed an elephant. But
> not the slightest mark was found on my devout head; and if I was
> to go round the country, and he with me, I exhibiting the stone as
> having fallen on me, and he as the man who would swear to it, I
> do not know which would be looked for with the most earnest-
> ness. However, it has been accepted by the jury. Now he says he
> only thinks so.

Speaking of the trials that followed, during which the unreliability of
many prosecution witnesses was revealed, he added:

> There is another matter to consider. I have been sworn to, I
> believe, by some of the witnesses who have also sworn to others,
> though some of them can prove they were in another city alto-
> gether—in Liverpool. Others have an overwhelming alibi, and I
> should by right have been tried with them; but I suppose your
> lordships cannot help that. We have, for instance, Thomas, the
> policeman, who swore to another prisoner. He identified him on a
> certain day, and the prisoner was not arrested for two days after-
> wards. As for Thomas, I do not presume that any jury could have
> believed him. He had heard of the blood-money and of course, was
> prepared to bid pretty high for it. My alibi has not been strong,
> and unfortunately I was not strong in pocket, and was not able to
> produce more testimony to prove where I was at exactly that time.
>
> With regard to the unfortunate man who has lost his life, I
> sympathise with him and his family as deeply as do your lordships

or the jury, or anyone in the court. I deeply regret the unfortunate occurrence, but I am as perfectly innocent of his blood as any man. I never had the slightest intention of taking life. I have done nothing at all in connection with that man, and I do not desire to be accused of a murder which I have not committed. With regard to another matter, my learned counsel has, no doubt for the best, expressed some opinions on the misgovernment to which my country has been subjected. I am firmly convinced there is prejudice in the minds of the people here, and it has been increased and excited by the newspapers, or by some of them, and to a certain extent has influenced the minds of the jury to convict the men standing in this dock, on a charge of which—a learned gentleman remarked a few nights since—they would be acquitted if they had been charged with murdering an old woman for the sake of the money in her pocket, but of a political offence of this kind they could not.

Now, sir, with regard to the opinions I hold on national matters —with regard to those men who have been released from that van, in which, unfortunately, life was lost, I believe that, certainly to some extent, there was an excuse. Perhaps it was unthought, but if those men had been in other countries, occupying other positions —if Jefferson Davis had been released in a northern city, there would have been a cry of applause throughout all England. If Garibaldi, whom I saw before I was shut out from the world, had been arrested, and was released, or something of that kind had taken place, they would have applauded the bravery of the act. If the captives of King Theodore had been released, that, too, would have been applauded. But, as it happened to be in England, of course, it is an awful thing, while yet in Ireland murders are perpetrated on unoffending men, as in the case of the riots in Waterford, where an unoffending man was murdered, and no one was punished for it. I do not desire to detain your lordships. I can only say that I leave this world without a stain on my conscience that I have been wilfully guilty of anything in connection with the death of Sergeant Brett. I am totally guiltless. I leave this world without malice to anyone. I do not accuse the jury, but I believe they were prejudiced. I do not accuse them of wilfully wishing to convict, but prejudice has induced them to convict when they otherwise would not have done it.

With reference to the witnesses, every one of them has sworn falsely. I never threw a stone or fired a pistol; I was never at the place, as they have said; it is all totally false. But as I have to go before my God, I forgive them. They will be able to meet me, some day, before that God Who is to judge us all, and then they and the people in this Court, and everyone, will know who tells the truth. Had I committed anything against the Crown of England, I would have scorned myself had I attempted to deny it; but with regard to these men, they have sworn what is altogether false. Had I been an Englishman, and arrested near the scene of that disturbance, I would have been brought as a witness to identify them; but, being an Irishman, it was supposed my sympathy was with them. On suspicion of that sympathy, I was arrested, and, in consequence of the arrest and the rewards which were offered, I was identified. It could not be otherwise. As I said before, my opinions on national matters do not at all relate to the case before your lordships. We have been found guilty, and, as a matter of course, we accept our death as gracefully as possible. We are not afraid to die—at least I am not.

"Nor I, nor I," repeated the other convicted men.

I have no sin or stain upon me; and I leave this world at peace with all. With regard to the other prisoners who are to be tried afterwards, I hope our blood at least will satisfy the craving for it. I hope our blood will be enough; and that those men, who I honestly believe are guiltless of the blood of that man,—that those other batches will get a fair, a free and more impartial trial. We view matters in a different light from what the jury do. We have been imprisoned, and have not had the advantage of understanding exactly to what this excitement has led. I can only hope and pray that this prejudice will disappear—that my oppressed country will right herself some day, and that her people, so far from being looked upon with scorn and aversion, will receive what they are entitled to, the respect not only of the civilised world, but of Englishmen.

I, too, am an American citizen, and on English territory I have committed no crime which makes me amenable to the Crown of England. I have done nothing; and, as a matter of course, I did expect protection—as this gentleman [pointing to O'Brien] has said, the protection of the Ambassador of my Government. I am a citizen of the State of Ohio; and I have to say my name is not

Shore. My name is Edward O'Meagher Condon. I belong to Ohio, and there are loving hearts there that will be sorry for this. I have nothing but my best wishes to send them, and my warmest feelings, and to assure them I can die as a Christian and an Irishman, and am not ashamed or afraid of anything I have done, or the consequences, before God or man. They would be ashamed of me if I was in the slightest degree a coward, or concealed my opinions.

In what must have been intended as an appeal for unity among the various Fenian factions in the United States, he came to that part of his speech which was to inspire Ireland in the same way that the rallying cry *"Eljen a Haza!"* (Long live our Country) had shouted defiance by the Magyars in the face of Austrian domination, a parallel drawn down the ages by perceptive men from Sydney Smith to Arthur Griffith.

> The unfortunate divisions of our countrymen in America have, to a certain extent, neutralised the efforts that we have made either in one direction or another for the liberation of our country. All these things have thwarted us, and as a matter of course we must only submit to our fate. I only trust again that those who are to be tried after us will have a fair trial, and that our blood will satisfy the cravings which I understand exist. You will soon send us before God, and I am perfectly prepared to go. I have nothing to regret, or to retract, or take back. I shall only say, GOD SAVE IRELAND!

At this point the words were taken up by his companions in the dock. "God save Ireland" they all cried. (It was these words which were taken up in the anthem which was to remain the National Anthem of Republicans until replaced by "The Soldiers' Song.") And then Condon added his few final words:

> I wish to add a word or two. There is nothing in the close of my political career which I regret. I don't know of one act which could bring the blush of shame to my face, or make me afraid to meet my God or fellowman. I would be most happy, and nothing would give me greater pleasure, than to die on the field for my country in defence of her liberty. As it is, I cannot die on the field, but I can die on the scaffold, I hope, as a soldier, a man and a Christian.

As the condemned men thanked their counsel, they looked towards the benches where their friends were seated and the only words that passed were perhaps the most moving of all: "God be with you, Irishmen and Irishwomen."

7

Aftermath

Ireland has never been short of martyrs, but there was a poignancy
about the history of Allen, Larkin and O'Brien which made their
execution the signal for an explosion of anger and revulsion against
British rule in Ireland. Echoes were heard in the United States and
even Australia. As M. Louis Blanc, correspondent for *Paris Temps*,
reported, the names of Allen, Larkin and O'Brien, "obscure names
belonging to oblivion", had become names which "Ireland will remember eternally thanks to yesterday's executions".

Commenting ironically on the alleged deterrent effect of the hangings, whose object was to intimidate would-be Fenians, he wrote:
"The proof that the authorities did not apprehend any attempt at
rescue—the proof that they were certain to inspire fear by hanging
these men—was their filling Manchester with troops," and he went on
to describe the elaborate precautions that had been taken.

Amazement, shock and horror were the reaction of the world's press,
while *The Times* (25th November) unswervingly defended the executions: "It has been said of a certain nation that they possess every virtue
under heaven except that of respect for law. . . . Never was an execution
less stimulated by the passion of bloodthirstiness." The Fenian's action
was a "crime against society" and had to be punished accordingly,
although "we do not attribute to the Manchester convicts the least
feeling of personal animosity against their victims".

The *Manchester Guardian* was concerned at the unpredictability of
Fenianism, speculating upon new "outrages in Vancouver and Hong
Kong".

But across the Irish Sea Press comment was bitter. The *Freeman's
Journal*, which had started by expressing concern at the incident, "A
strange if not alarming illustration of the extent of the organisation, and
of the capacity of those who direct it" (19th September), commented
on 25th November on the martyrdom of Allen, O'Brien, and
Larkin:

They were humble Irishmen, and they fearlessly suffered for a cause they believed to be true. It would be a foolish as well as dangerous delusion to make light of the motives that brought these men to the scaffold. There can be no doubt that thousands in England and Ireland would welcome death in the same cause as steadily as Allen, O'Brien and Larkin. Whatever men may think of it—they may call it folly, madness, or anything they please—there it is, the most widely spread and unmanageable social malady with which England ever had to deal. And England deals with it in a fashion which, so far from removing or conquering, will only root it more deeply and diffuse it more widely. It is not by blood it can be cured. The gibbet is a bad doctor and always was . . .

We have no desire to revive past animosities, but we must say that no policy tends so much to re-create discord and hate as the sacrifice of Saturday. It was not a display of strength, but of *weakness* instigated by anger and fear!

From the *Journal's* Special Correspondent in Manchester came the comment:

It was rather remarkable that the Home Secretary doubted "the propriety" of the conviction—and more curious still that he should have refused to reserve the question raised by prisoner's counsel, because it had been considered with the utmost care and gravity by the judges. These judges had "fully concurred" in the death sentence on the five men, and if that awful opinion were found not only revocable, but substantially wrong, surely their judgement in another matter might with decency have been reviewed and investigated. It is a sad fact that Mr. Hardy's notion of etiquette should deprive death-doomed men of even a chance of reprieve—while Mr. Adams' conception of the rights of an American citizen set aside in the face of an angry nation the deliberate judgement of the English Crown.

The Nation issued a black-bordered edition on 30th November, and *The Irish Catholic Chronicle and Peoples News of the Week*, a Dublin periodical, set the tone of much of the Irish Press in its editorial of 30th November:

Mankind indeed will be apt to characterise by the foul name of murder, not the casual death of the policeman, but the deliberate and dastardly slaughter of the Fenian victims. At all events Irishmen can have but one feeling regarding this odious crime, and all who have committed, advised, abetted, or rejoiced at it. Nor is it a feeling that will quickly pass away. In that miserable five minutes on the scaffold of Manchester a deed was done that has sundered Englishmen and Irishmen for this generation. "There rolls between us a great sea of blood." In one day the political relations between the two countries have retrograded half a century.

It is ironical that almost half a century later, the 1916 executions were to create the climate of opinion that lead to the creation of the Free State and the Republic and that DeValera, as an American citizen, was pardoned—a remarkable parallel with the Manchester executions and the pardoning of Condon.

The *Kilkenny Journal* asserted that the men had been hanged for political reasons.

The *Dundalk Democrat* commented that the crime was not murder, as it was not premeditated; further, it was a political crime; to hang them would be a blow to the cause of law and order. It was not unlikely that these men would be looked upon as martyrs and Fenians would seek to avenge their death.

The *Tipperary and Clare Independent* said they had been "murdered by law". They were not guilty of wilful murder, nor was the procedure and manner of trial above suspicion.

The *Munster News* thought that the carrying-out of sentences would increase the power of Fenianism and create sympathy where once this was non-existent or dormant.

The *Cork Examiner* described the executions as ". . . a sacrifice to the spirit and hatred and brutal revenge".

The *Ulster Observer* stated that ". . . on the scaffold at Manchester three men have been sacrificed to the Moloch of anti-Irish prejudice and English hostility." Its editorial commented scathingly that the prisoners had been convicted by the English Press before the trial ever took place, and that

the majesty of the law and the thirst of the English rabble for blood —a thirst incited and sustained by a truculent and brutal press— have been vindicated and gratified, and the Irish heart has received a further accession to its long heritage of hate. When other nations —when even Russia and Turkey blush to have recourse to capital punishment for what are called political offenders, who are after all but the vanguard of future freedom—England, the arch-hypocrite of the nations, with liberty on her lips and tyranny in her heart and in her deeds, submits to the fate of the vilest felon men who before any other tribunal on earth would be acquitted of any crime greater than a street riot with violence.

The *Waterford Citizen* considered that the conduct of the trial was characterised by blundering, cruelty and foreknowledge of the verdict. The *Tipperary Vindicator* published an editorial in which it said that

> Their death may have gratified the passion of England for a brief space of time, but its ultimate result will be to intensify her troubles, and it may be to awaken her remorse. They were poor and uninfluential men—she has made them great. They were weak —she has made them potent as an army. They were neither agitators, nor poets, nor orators—she has given to the last few words that escaped their lips an eloquence unparalleled, a power that thrills and sways the hearts of millions of men at this moment, and that will continue to exercise the same charm on the Irish heart for all time. Their simple yet glorious prayer for their country already has an ominous sound to the ears of England; who can say how soon it may become to her guilty conscience a word of terror?

The English Radical *Reynolds News* on 24th November commented that if justice rather than panic had influenced the actions of the Government, the testimony at the trial "would not hang a cat".

John Bright later commented that he believed the three men were hanged because it was a political offence, and not for an ordinary murder of one man by one man by one shot.

Frederick Engels condemned the execution, comparing it with the execution of John Brown following the attack on Harper's ferry,[1] stating that "The Fenians could not wish for a better precedent." He considered it to be

> the definite deed of separation between England and Ireland. . . . All the Fenians lacked was Martyrs. . . . Through the execution of these men the liberation of Kelly and Deasy has been made an act of heroism which will now be sung over the cradle of every Irish child. The Irish women will take care of that.

Across the Atlantic the thunder rolled as, on 9th December, the *New York Herald* gave its verdict:

> The death of those men will create a profound sensation throughout the civilized world, while the reckless and hopeless attempts of

---

[1] Engels, *Briefwechsel*, iii, 449.

the Fenians to excite a rebellion against the British Government are
to be deplored as only tending to destroy human life and to
increase the sufferings of the oppressed Irish people. England will
meet with little sympathy from other nations in her domestic
troubles. When the position she took during our own rebellion is
remembered, the United States might well be justified in condemning her severity towards her own political offenders as
barbarous and brutal. . . . Whether the triple execution will lay the
terrible Fenian ghost in Ireland and England remains to be seen. It
may check any more outbreaks for awhile, but it is not at all
improbable that it may rankle in the minds of the masses, and in
the end bring forth even more bitter fruit than the tree of Fenianism has yet produced.

The *New York Times* considered that the trial was unfair, stating:

Looking at the black record of Ireland's wrongs for centuries, we
must agree with the English Reform League in avowing sympathy
with, and commiseration for, those who have been goaded into
violence by the accumulated crimes of the British Government.

The Continental Press added to the general condemnation. "The
executions may cost dearly to an aristocratic Government," wrote
Liberté, while *Independence Belge* added that: "the execution, of which
the Government and the Queen has assumed the heavy responsibility,
is to be much deplored".

Many, who had until the day of the execution stood aloof from
Fenianism, were awakened to the nature of their rulers. Executions
have always been good recruiting grounds for the cause they were
calculated to extinguish and Britain was to repeat its terror, fatally for
the Union, in 1916. In 1867, the deaths of Allen, Larkin and O'Brien
saw the birth of a new spirit which was to put the Irish Question at
the centre of British politics for more than half a century.

Ten years later, when Sir Michael Hicks Beach described the
prisoners as "the Manchester murderers" Parnell exclaimed from the
Irish benches: "No! no!" "I regret," said Mr. Hicks Beach, "that there
is any Honourable Member in this House who will apologise for
murder." Mr. Parnell rose in his seat and replied: "The Right Honourable Gentleman looked at me so directly when he said he regretted that
any member of this House should apologise for murder that I wish to
say as publicly and as directly as I can that I do not believe, and never
shall believe, that any murder was committed at Manchester."

Michael Davitt was to express the same view years later, but added that no death would have occurred had he been at the scene.

Certainly the reaction in Radical and Fenian circles to the news of the executions indicated the same belief. Demonstrations in the form of funeral processions took place in many parts of the world.

The execution dug a gulf between England and Ireland which is only now being bridged, a century later. The intensity of passion which it provoked is still reflected among the descendants of the Manchester Irish who have learned the story of the Martyrs from their fathers and mothers. It is part of the folklore of Manchester and there are many who claim to be descended from participants in the incident. It gave birth to many a ballad and many a story. Colonel Kelly's grand-niece lives in Oranmore, Co. Galway, where a memorial has recently been erected at Mount Bellew. Her sister resides in New York and another distant relative lives in London. All have had the story of the rescue handed down to them and have added to the information available.

Explosive passions were unleashed by the ultimate act of retribution at Salford gaol. When *The Times* complained that the demonstrators "converted a ceremonial otherwise religious into a parade of political hatred" it was stating no more than the truth.

But one procession which bridged the gulf was that planned before the executions from Clerkenwell to Hyde Park. It manifested the sympathy and solidarity of ordinary Englishmen with their Irish fellows. There were at least some who understood the basic unity of interest between English and Irish in removing the oppression of those who ruled them both.

Mr. Finlan at that historic demonstration "prayed that the blood so wantonly and unnecessarily shed would tend to cement and consolidate the sympathies and hearts of English, Irish and Scots in one holy and invincible bond, dedicated to the regeneration of these Islands, afflicted as they were by class despotism, dishonour and class slavery".

In Manchester itself nearly 3,000 men and women marched through the streets, in pouring rain, watched by 5,000 to 6,000 spectators. No police were in evidence and there was no disturbance on the route from Stevenson Square—scene of many a subsequent political clash in the 1930s—to New Cross. Many wore green, and crosses and shamrocks were much in evidence among the well dressed orderly marchers.

In many towns and cities demonstrations or funeral processions were banned by the local Magistrates. Such was the case in Glasgow and Newcastle, while in Liverpool local Orangemen threatened a counter-march if a procession for the Manchester Martyrs was held.

In Cork 12,000 marchers in "perfect order and sobriety" demonstrated their grief at the death of their compatriots. At about two o'clock the procession began to form up opposite the Mercy Hospital. At the head of the cortège was an empty bier drawn by four horses in sable trappings. A train of women and girls, wearing green ribands and rosettes and signs of mourning, followed the cortège. After these were the boys of the charity schools, wearing crêpe bands on their caps; then came the tailors, shoemakers, masons, carpenters, joiners, working engineers, stonecutters, plasterers and other sections of workers, walking in procession three-deep followed by a large variety of the ordinary people of Cork. Thousands more witnessed the procession, displaying obvious sympathy at what was regarded generally as a demonstration against the Government.

The most remarkable of the demonstrations took place in Dublin on Sunday, 8th December. On that day the Fenians peacefully controlled the streets of Ireland's capital city. Again marching in the rain they wore green ribands, bonnets and sashes and displayed the harp and the shamrock. After the thousands of processionists came three hearses, followed by mourning coaches and cabs.

Behind the first Mr. John Martin walked with Mr. A. M. Sullivan as chief mourner. The hearses bore the names of Allen, O'Brien and Larkin on drapes suspended at each side. As the procession wound through the Dublin streets fresh marchers joined in from every side. Eleven bands took part in the procession, playing funeral airs, and on every pavement and at the windows stood sympathisers. The *Manchester Guardian* estimated 15–30,000 participants. Some put the figure at as much as 80,000.

Mr. Martin's funeral oration captured the mood of the Irish people after the executions:

> Now it has come to pass, as a consequence of the malignant policy pursued for so many long years, that the great body of the Irish people despair of obtaining peaceful restitution of our national rights. And it has also come to pass that vast numbers of Irishmen whom the oppression of English rule forbade to live by honest industry in their own country have in America learned to become soldiers. Those Irish soldiers seem resolved to make war against England, and England is in a panic of rage and fear in consequence.
> This demonstration is mainly one of mourning for the fate of

those three good Irishmen, but it is also one of protest and indignation against the conduct of our alien rulers. She has committed
such an outrage on justice and decency as to make many Englishmen stand aghast.

The troops stationed in the city were confined to their barracks but
kept in readiness for action. On the same day processions took place at
Limerick, Middleton, Skibbereen and Mitchelstown. Many more were
banned by the authorities.

As a result of his articles and cartoons relating to the Manchester
executions in the *Weekly News*, Mr. A. M. Sullivan was placed on trial
and sentenced to six months' imprisonment at Richmond. Richard
Pigott also stood trial for articles in *The Irishman*. At his trial Sullivan
reaffirmed his belief in the innocence of the Martyrs:

> Yes, in that hour they told us they were innocent but were ready
> to die, and we believed them. We believe them still. They did not
> go to their God with falsehood on their lips. What we contend is
> that the men in Manchester would never have been found guilty
> on such evidence, would never have been executed on such a
> verdict, if time had been given to let panic and passion pass away.

Preparations for a rally at Liverpool, announced by Mr. A. J. O'Shea,
were thwarted by threats of violence from the local Orangemen. But
in Birmingham, the *Birmingham Daily Post* reported that 2,500 people
assembled on the slopes of St. Joseph's Cemetery; green ribbons,
rosettes and crêpe stood out as a portion of the Roman Catholic Litany
was read to the assembled crowd.

Hussars and artillery stood by at Leeds, and in towns like Bolton,
Warrington, Davenport, Plymouth, Sunderland, Glasgow, Lancaster,
Rochdale, Litchfield, Newcastle, Wolverhampton, and even on the
Isle of Wight, no procession was allowed to take place. But in Allen's
home town of Bandon a procession of mourners from miles around
passed for prayers at his family home and at the local convent.

That the evils of English rule in Ireland were highlighted by the
men of Manchester there can be no doubt, for although the subsequent
ill-advised attempt to blow up Clerkenwell Prison to free two other
Fenians, Burke and Casey, was to cause a wave of resentment against
Fenianism because of the loss of innocent life, nevertheless even Gladstone himself, when he came to Lancashire in December, felt it necessary to allude to Ireland. After a fierce denunciation of Fenian outrages,

some of which it must be conceded, like Clerkenwell, showed a fearful disregard for the need to enlist sympathetic opinion in England, he went on: "Yet . . . we must not forget to ask ourselves whether the condition of Ireland is such as it ought to be, whether we have put ourselves in the right, whether we have given to that country the full benefit of equal principles and legislation and if we find we are not able to assert that of ourselves, we must not be ashamed to endeavour to put ourselves in the right, we must not be ashamed to confess it when we have done wrong."[1] Two decades were to pass before Gladstone was himself converted to the idea of Home Rule.

The strength of feeling manifested in England and Ireland was reflected across the Atlantic, where the Senate Wing of the Fenian Movement were to carry out some remarkable but often naïve escapades in the years to come. The *New York Herald* reported: "One of the most imposing gatherings that the Fenians of this city ever had. . . . Like a serpent of chameleon hue the procession defiled along Chatham Square down towards the hall of the city and like an army it marched across the park in review order by the Mayor and Corporation, who stood on the steps of the City Hall to receive them."

At the head of the procession was carried a placard bearing the following inscription:

> Whether on the scaffold high
> Or in the battle van,
> The fittest place for man to die
> Is when he dies for man.

*   *   *

The smashing of the van was perhaps the high-water-mark of Fenian activity in England, a wave which struck at England's shores in the wake of the failure of 1867. And while it is not the purpose of this account to do more than scratch the surface of Fenianism as a movement, it may be said that this episode reflected the strength and weakness of Fenianism.

It demonstrated audacity, courage and reckless disregard for self: it demonstrated the strength of feeling among ordinary Irishmen and their ability to match radical words with hot deeds. It demonstrated also the lack of perspective and long-term planning. It demonstrated the fundamental weakness to this day of most Irish national movements in failing to recognise their problem as part of a whole rather than as

[1] Oldham, 18th December, 1867, reported in *Manchester Guardian*, 19th December.

something unique. True, from Wolfe Tone to James Connolly there were those who were influenced by European thought, and the liberal revolutions of 1848 found their reflection in Ireland. But all too often Irish political groups in general and Fenianism in particular were a specifically Irish phenomenon, trying to find solutions to their problems in isolation.

Irishmen in England sometimes broke through these fetters, and O'Connell was one such giant. There were bonds of sympathy which in Mr. Richardson's words at Clerkenwell produced a situation in which "The men of London could leave their homes on such a night to speak in mercy's name . . . to stay the tyranny of any Government however bloodthirsty it might be, to save the lives of those misguided, rash but patriotic men of Manchester."

But there should have been more, and part of the fault lies not only with the chauvinist attitudes of many Englishmen in a century when Britannia really did rule the waves and the British Empire had pushed itself to the furthest extremities of the globe. Separated by geography, history and religion from England and therefore from much of liberal and socialist thought developing in industrial Britain, there was a tendency in Ireland to see things in isolation. Links were more frequent with the New World of the United States, where Fenianism was to exist in one form or another throughout the century. Irish radicalism before Davitt had too few links with radical or socialist thought, whether of a scientific or utopian character. There was perhaps too little emphasis on the social problems and the overriding need for land reform. It had more than a little in common with the action theories of anarchists, but it was nationalism rather than internationalism which dictated both ideals and methods. Certainly only men with a limited understanding of common problems and aims could be guilty of such a grave error as the Clerkenwell affair following the arrest of Ricard O'Sullivan Burke whose dealings in arms with a Liverpool gunsmith had been revealed by the spy Corydon. The indiscriminate killing of innocent people passing by the prison when it was dynamited could only alienate public opinion and set back the Irish cause.

An element of political infantilism comes into the attempts to invade Canada. But up until the execution of the Manchester Martyrs and beyond, Fenianism with all its weakness represented the most radical and determined attempt to rid Ireland of its historical oppressors. While Parnell and the Parliamentary Party have proved of great and unending interest to historians, it is from the Fenians that the inspiration for the eventual liberators of Ireland came, and it is to the Fenians that one must look for the precursors of many a successful nationalist movement in the twentieth century. The liberation of Kelly and Deasy, and the subsequent trial and execution, must not be looked at as a meaningless though exciting stage in the history of England and Ireland, but as a microcosm of a problem and situation in which all the elements of the complex relationship were present, and in which the role of the expatriate colonial in a metropolitan country was transformed from the passive provider of labour-power to the front ranks of the struggle for his nation's assertion of independence.

It is not without significance that on 22nd November, 1879, when the newly-formed Land League supported by Parnell and Davitt sent an army of 8,000 men armed with sticks and blackthorns to prevent the eviction of the Dempsey family, banners were carried with the inscription "In memoriam, Allen, Larkin and O'Brien", as the next day was the anniversary of their execution. Thus, the Manchester execution still served as an inspiration to the newly militant movement for agrarian reform and to Irish emancipation under a very different type of leadership with methods far removed from the secretive character of Fenianism.

In a letter dated 13th December, 1913, Joseph McGarrity, a generation later, wrote:[1] "You will see in the 'Gaelic American' what was done in Dublin to commemorate the anniversary of the deaths of Allen, Larkin and O'Brien. It was a magnificent demonstration—the finest of its kind I have ever witnessed." The Manchester Martyrs were still the inspiration of the radical wing of the Irish Movement and their names carried a magic that would inspire the Irish volunteers in the final years of Ireland's struggle to free itself from English rule.

As such they constitute one of the most fascinating episodes to nineteenth-century history with some lessons for those striving to solve the problems posed by the Partition of Ireland which remain with us a century later. It was the spirit of the Fenians that won through in 1916 and another martyrdom was to sustain the tide which led to the establishment of the Republic.

"But that spirit is not dead but merely sleepeth, and if there be men still in Ireland, and more, boys growing into men, willing to strive and struggle and sacrifice if needs be, liberty or life for Ireland, to Fenianism more than ought else is that spirit and feeling due."[2]

[1] "Clann na Gael and the I.R.B.", by Sean Cronin, *Irish Times*, 19th April, 1969.
[2] O'Leary, *Recollections*, 1896, Vol. II, pp. 242–3.

8

Postscript

Today the memory of the three men is enshrined in stone at St. Joseph's Cemetery, Moston, Manchester. Surrounded by a grass verge and only a few yards from the main entrance to the right, their monument is the scene of an annual ceremony of remembrance. Somewhat weather-beaten now, the grey stone carvings sum up the intense national feeling of those Irishmen and women who, forced by poverty and hunger from their native land, settled in Manchester in the nineteenth century.

The *Manchester City News* of 20th March, 1897, announced the placing of the memorial in Moston cemetery. The foundation stone was laid by Mr. James Stephens, head of the Fenian Movement thirty-one years before, the same James Stephens rescued by Colonel Kelly—the wheel had turned full circle.

> The memorial [wrote the *City News*] takes the form of a Celtic Cross some twenty feet high which is to be placed on a lofty pedestal. The foundation stone is from the Hill of Tara, the base of the memorial will be composed of sixteen stones representing the counties of Ireland, and the corner stones represent the four Irish provinces. In front of the cross is the figure of Erin armed with sword and shield and on the reverse a miniature copy of an Irish round tower. At each corner there is to be a figure of an Irish wolf-hound, and the portraits of the three men are to be given. The memorial has been designed and will be carried out by Mr. J. Geraghty of Bootle. The laying of the foundation stone was made the occasion of an imposing public demonstration in the city. Deputations of Irishmen being present from most of the large towns of Lancashire and Yorkshire. After the ceremony a meeting was held in St. James's Hall Mr. E. Griffin presiding.

In 1903, the Manchester Martyrs Central Memorial Committee added to the memorial by open subscription, so that the surrounds of the monument are now turfed and enclosed. To Seamus Barnett (1857–1943), now buried close to the monument, goes much of the credit for keeping "the memories evergreen of the boys who smashed the van". Every year the men are remembered at Easter time in a service and ceremony in the city and by the graveside: the author was accorded a privilege unique to a non-Irishman in addressing the annual gathering in 1966.

As for the Martyrs themselves, when the New Bailey Prison was pulled down, their remains were transferred to Strangeways. Only their letters remain to remind us of the poignancy of this event which took place a century ago.

Deasy died early in 1880 but Kelly was to honour the Martyrs together with O'Sullivan Burke as late as 1903 in New York. Kelly, who worked in the New York Custom House, died on 5th February, 1908, and was buried at Woodlawn Cemetery. Married twice, he had two daughters by his first wife, who ran a hotel called 'The Log Cabin' in Atlantic City. His second wife, Anna, bore him a son. On Kelly's grave is the inscription: "Thomas J. Kelly, Civil War Veteran 1861–66, Grand Army of the Republic, New York City". Anna lived until 1913. Kelly's Reports are among the O'Donovan Rossa papers held in New York and may well yield up a valuable insight into the work of Irish-American Fenians. There is, however, some evidence that Kelly was involved in an incursion over the Canadian border in 1871 when the Canadian Custom House at Pembina was temporarily overcome and recaptured.

In Saint Patrick's Church, Livesey Street, Manchester, the last letter from Michael O'Brien is still preserved.

NEW BAILEY PRISON, SALFORD,
November 14th, 1867.

MY DEAR BROTHER,—I have been intending to write to you for some time, but having seen a letter from Mr. Moore, addressed to the Governor of this prison, and knowing from it that you must be in a disagreeable state of suspense, I may therefore let you know how I am at once. With reference to the trial and all connected with it, it was unfair from beginning to end; and if I should die in consequence, it will injure my murderers more than it will injure me. Why should I fear to die, innocent as I am of the charge which a prejudiced jury, assisted by perjured witnesses, found me guilty of? I will do judge and jury the justice of saying they believed me guilty of being—a citizen of the United States, a friend to liberty, a hater of relentless cruelty, and therefore no friend to the British

Government, as it exists in our beautiful island. I must say, much though I would like to live, that I cannot regret dying in the cause of Liberty and Ireland. It has been made dear to me by the sufferings of its people, by the martyrdom and exile of its best and noblest sons. The priest, the scholar, the soldier, the saint have suffered and died proudly, nobly; and why should I shrink from death in a cause made holy and glorious by the members of its martyrs and the heroism of its supporters, as well as by its justice? You don't, and never shall, forget that Peter O'Neill Crowley died only a short time since in this cause.

> "Far dearer the grave or the prison,
> Illum'd by one patriot name,
> Than the trophies of all who have risen
> On liberty's ruins to fame."

I should feel ashamed of my manhood if I thought myself capable of doing anything mean to save my life, to get out of here, or for any other selfish purpose. Let no man think a cause is lost because some suffer for it. It is only a proof that those who suffer are in earnest, and should be an incentive to others to be equally so —to do their duty with firmness, justice and disinterestedness. I feel as confident of the ultimate success of the Irish cause as I do of my own existence. God, in His great mercy and goodness, will strengthen the arm of the patriot, and give him wisdom to free his country. Let us hope that He, in His wisdom, is only trying our patience. The greater its sufferings, the more glorious will He make the future of our unfortunate country and its people.

The shriek of the famine-stricken mother and the helpless infant as well as the centuries of misery call to Heaven for vengeance. God is slow, but just! The blood of Tone, Fitzgerald, Emmet and others has been shed—how much good has it done the tyrant and the robber? None. Smith, O'Brien, MacManus and Mitchel suffered for Ireland, yet not their sufferings, nor those of O'Donovan Rossa and his companions, deterred Burke, MacAfferty and their friends from doing their duty. Neither shall the sufferings of my companions, nor mine, hinder my countrymen from taking their part in the inevitable struggle, but rather nerve their arms to strike.

I would write on this subject at greater length, but I hope that I have written enough to show you that if a man dies for liberty, his memory lives in the breasts of the good and virtuous. You will also see that there is no necessity for my father, mother, sisters or relations fretting about me. When I leave this world, it will be (with God's help) to go to a better, to join the angels and saints of God, and sing His praises for all eternity. I leave a world of sufferings for one of eternal joy and happiness. I have been to Holy Communion, and, please God, intend going shortly again. I am sorry we cannot hear Mass; the good priest is not allowed to say it in this prison.

Give my love to my father and mother, to Mary, Ellen, John Philips, Tim, Catherine, uncles, aunts and cousins.

Farewell.

From your affectionate Brother,

MICHAEL O'BRIEN (alias WILLIAM GOULD)

At the National Museum in Dublin is a stone which is claimed to be the very one used to smash in the top of the van. It was presented by the Reverend Rupert in 1935. A drawing of the attack on the van by Bolgar, the man whose criticism provoked O'Meagher Condon's account, is also kept there. Also preserved is the last letter of William Philip Allen, written on the day before his execution.

SALFORD NEW BAILEY PRISON,
November 22nd, 1867.

TO YOU, MY LOVING AND SINCERE DEAR UNCLE AND AUNT,

I suppose this is my last letter to you at this side of the grave. Oh, dear Uncle and Aunt, if you reflect on it, it is nothing. I am dying an honourable death; I am dying for Ireland—dying for the land that gave me birth—dying for the Island of Saints—and dying for liberty. Every generation of our countrymen has suffered; and where is the Irish heart could stand by unmoved? I should like to know what trouble, what passion, what mischief could separate the true Irish heart from its own native isle. Dear Uncle and Aunt, it is sad to be parting with you all, at my early age; but we must all die some day or another. A few hours more, and I will breathe my last, and on English soil. Oh, that I could be buried in Ireland! What a happiness it would be to all my friends, and to myself— Where my countrymen could kneel on my grave. I cannot express what joy it afforded me, when I found Aunt Sarah and you were admitted. Dear Uncle, I am sure it was not a very pleasant place I had to receive yourself and my aunt; but we must put up with all trials until we depart this life. I am sure it will grieve you very much to leave me in such a place, on the evidence of such characters as the witnesses were that swore my life away. But I forgive them, and may God forgive them. I am dying, thank God! an Irishman and a Christian. Give my love to all friends; same from your ever affectionate nephew.

Pray for us. Good-bye and remember me. Good-bye and may heaven protect you all, is the last wish of your dying nephew.

W. P. Allen

A hundred years later, in April, 1967, the *Dungannon Observer* published the following remarkable report from Pittsburg, a city very much like Manchester on the other side of the Atlantic Ocean:

LETTERS OF MANCHESTER
MARTYRS FOUND IN
PITTSBURG, U.S.A.

WILLIAM P. ALLEN'S FAREWELL MESSAGES TO FAMILY PRESENTED TO LIBRARY OF IRISH CENTRE

By Tom McGuigan Jr.

I was present in the home of Mr. Robert Gariby, great grand-nephew of William P. Allen, one of the three Manchester Martyrs (Allen, Larkin and O'Brien), when Mr. Gariby turned over to Dr. James McKaveney five letters which were written by Allen to members of his family on the eve of his execution. These letters will be hermetically encased, and put on permanent display in the library of the new Irish Centre in Pittsburg, Pa.

The following is transcribed from one of these missives that have come to light in this, the Centenary of The Manchester Martyrs.

New Bailey Prison,
Salford,
November 20, 1867.

My Dear Uncle and Aunt O'Brien—It afforded me much pleasure, I can assure you, in seeing poor Uncle John, Ellen, Michael, John and Mary Anne today. Their hands I shook, their lips I kissed, will I ever kiss them or shake their hands again? I should like to see Uncle James, Aunt Mary and Uncle Michael, if you could come to see me. I received a letter on Tuesday evening from your Uncle James, which pleased me very much; I was sorry to hear my Aunt

Mary was not well. I really love poor Aunt Mary and Ellen Quin, and let you all be fond of them for my sake; for the sake of a true and noble hearted nephew. There is a namesake of ours here, in the cell opposite me, Michael O'Brien, lying also under sentence of death. May God help him, and help us all. If it is the will of God we should go to the scaffold, we will have the prayers and good-will of many a thousand that never saw us; and many a tear shall flow from the hearts of the true and the brave. Give my love to all my inquiring friends. It is hard to say Mary Anne Hickey is not allowed in. Uncle James you try and come to see me. I should like to see John. No more at present from your loving and affectionate nephew.   Wm. P. Allen

Good bye cousin Mary Anne, the last kiss.

In the same month as this discovery, the English *Daily Mail* was was to report on "a plan by left-wing Irish patriots to place in an English city (Manchester) what critics have described as 'a memorial to murderers'", thus raising anew the controversy that shook Manchester a century earlier. It is a strange irony that while Britain can honour President Kenyatta only a few years after his imprisonment for alleged Mau Mau activities and publish a stamp in honour of Gandhi's centen-ary, Allen, Larkin and O'Brien can still arouse angry passions a century later. As I write these lines the shock waves still resound as Civil Rights Marchers in Derry join hands with English liberals and socialists in what may be the last chapter of a story in which the Fenians and the tragedy of the Manchester Martyrs played such an ounstanding part. The common bond of English and Irish history will one day overcome the fears and hatreds of the past in a recognition of the fact that those who persecuted Ireland were also the exploiters of their own com-patriots. The names of Ernest Jones and the men of Clerkenwell will be remembered when the gallows are a forgotten relic of the past.

It remains only to add that Sergeant Brett's remains lie in the Harpurhey cemetery not far from Moston, his tombstone bearing the words, "I will do my duty", and a memorial tablet graces St. Anne's Church in the fashionable centre of Manchester. It is rumoured that until recently the prison van was rotting in a garden at Eccles but none of those interested have been able to locate it. Time has probably taken its toll, and while neither the Fenian Arch nor their prison remain, the Fenians' story will ever be part of the history of Ireland's struggle to be both Gaelic and Free.

Ballads of the Manchester Martyrs

THE SMASHING OF THE VAN

ATTEND, you gallant Irishmen, and listen for a while:
I'll sing to you the praises of the sons of Erin's Isle.
It's of those gallant heroes who voluntarily ran
To release two Irish Fenians from an English prison van.

CHORUS
Hurrah, my lads, for freedom, let all join heart and hand!
May the Lord have mercy on the boys that helped to smash the van!

On the Eighteenth of September, it was a dreadful year,
When sorrow and excitement ran all through Lancashire.
At a gathering of the Irish boys they volunteered each man.
To release those Irish prisoners from out of the prison van.

Kelly and Deasy were their names. I suppose you know them well;
Remanded for a week they were in Belle Vue Gaol to dwell.
When taking of the prisoners back, their trial for to stand,
To make a safe deliverance they conveyed them in a van.

William Deasy was a man of good and noted fame
Likewise Michael Larkin, we'll ne'er forget his name;
With young Allen and O'Brien they took a part so grand
In that glorious liberation and the smashing of the van.

In Manchester one morning these heroes did agree
Their leaders, Kelly and Deasy, should have their liberty:
They drank a health to Ireland, and soon made up the plan.
To meet the prisoners on the road and take and smash the van.

With courage bold those heroes went, and soon the van did stop;
They cleared the guards from back and front, and then smashed
    in the top;
But when blowing open of the lock they chanced to kill a man.
So three must die on the scaffold high for smashing of the van.

I

One cold November morning in Eighteen Sixty-seven,
These martyrs to their country's cause a sacrifice were given.
"God save Ireland!" was their cry, all through the crowd it ran.
The Lord have mercy on the boys that helped to smash the van!

> So now kind friends, I will conclude; I think it would be right
> That all true-hearted Irishmen together should unite;
> Together should unite, my friends, and do the best we can
> To keep the memory ever green of the boys that smashed the van.

GOD SAVE IRELAND

HIGH upon the gallows tree swung the noble-hearted three
  By the vengeful tyrant stricken in their bloom;
But they met him face to face, with the courage of their race,
  And they went with soul undaunted to their doom.

CHORUS
"God save Ireland," said the heroes;
  "God save Ireland," said they all.
"Whether on the scaffold high or on battlefield we die
  O what matter when for Erin dear we fall."

Girt around with cruel foes, still their courage proudly rose,
  For they thought of hearts that loved them far and near;
Of the millions true and brave o'er the ocean's swelling wave
  And the friends in holy Ireland ever dear.

Climbed they up the rugged stair, rang their voices out in prayer,
  Then with England's fatal cord around them cast,
Close beside the gallows tree, they kissed like brothers lovingly,
  True to home and faith and freedom to the last.

Never till the latest day shall the memory pass away
  Of the gallant lives thus given for our land;
But on the cause must go, amid joy or weal or woe,
  Till we make our isle a nation free and grand.

T. D. SULLIVAN

ALLEN, LARKIN AND O'BRIEN

GOD rest the dead of Ireland
  Who sleep in Irish clay!
God rest the dead of Ireland
  Whose graves are far away!
God rest the noble Martyred Three
  Whose names like a beacon shine
To lead us on till the goal is won—
  Allen, Larkin and O'Brien.

Because they loved their Motherland
  And strove to set her free,
The lash of England's hate came down
  On the brave undaunted three.
And, comrades all in Ireland's cause
  The task is yours and mine
To break one day the hand that smote
  Allen, Larkin and O'Brien.

They heard no call of pipe or drum,
  No comrades marched ahead,
But round them were the spirit hosts
  Of Ireland's martyred dead.
With heads erect and hearts aglow
  They joined that sainted line,
Dear Ireland's name on their dying lips
  Allen, Larkin and O'Brien.

Their cause is Ireland's cause today,
  Their foe is Ireland's foe.
The fires they lit of love and hate,
  Bright, bright and warm they glow;
And where their flame lights up the sky
  We read the blood-red sign
That tells of vengeance for our dead—
  Allen, Larkin and O'Brien.

                    BRIAN NA BANBAN

THE MANCHESTER MARTYRS

(The author of this poem—an Irish journalist working in England
—was present at the martyrdom of Allen, Larkin and O'Brien, at
Salford Prison, Manchester, 23rd November, 1867.)

THERE are three graves in England newly dug,
    In England there are three men less today—
Allen, O'Brien, Larkin—their brief sun has set,
    To rise in God's clear day.

I saw them, the unconquerable Three,
    Mount the black gallows for their country's faith,
As with the high heroic scorn of life they kissed
    The frozen lips of death.

Earth reeled in darkness as one after one,
    Knitted like steel, passed up the sloping stair,
And in their eyes and in their faces shone
    The hope that shames despair.

Below, the turbulent, fierce multitude
    Glared at the Martyrs wildly; but they stood
Willing for Ireland and her trampled cause
    To shed their hearts' last blood.

The thick November fog came up and rolled
    A vivid light around each defiant head;
Ah! not at Marathon or Bannockburn
    Have braver soldiers bled.

The thin, pale face of Allen, O'Brien's gaze,
    And Larkin, fainting from the press of doom,
Seemed like the Trinity of Ireland's trust
    In that foul morning's gloom.

'Twas over, and they fell; one little pause,
    And the sun, battling with the mist, broke out,
And with a glory to November new,
    He hemmed them round about.

Even the passionate pallor of the crowd
    Crimsoned into a pity, as the Three,
Smitten by the Empire's sword of rope,
    Passed to Eternity.

THE MANCHESTER MARTYRS

AYE, stand them high on your gallows tree!
    Where the noose of a hangman waits,
And the ribald cries of your rabble rise
    Outside of their prison gates;
Let them stand in the light of your murky skies
    So the nations of men may see
How Ireland offers a sacrifice
    On the altars of liberty.

The world has plenty of mouthed wars
    And aims that the gods despise;
Was ever a victory blessed by Mars
    Achieved by a braggart's cries?—
No. The hero's blood and the bullet's hum
    Are the liberty's pangs of birth,
And by these must be settled the awful sum
    Of tyranny's debt to earth.

Then stand them high with their eyes to the light,
    Those sons of a soldier race;
Each strand of their halters marks their right
    To glory's innermost place;
And their "God Save Ireland" proudly hurled
    From the portals of death will fling
Its echoes forever around the world
    While the soul of the Celt is king.

This day will end at the setting of sun,
    But the fame of our noble Three
Will live till the uttermost sands are run
    Of the Land that they died to free;

The justice of God is lightning-shod,
  And tyrants pass in a day;
But the martyr's blood and the hero's sword
  Will be saviours of men for aye.

And not for the Land of their birth alone
  Do they swing from your beams of shame,
But for every struggle the world has known,
  In Liberty's holy name;
For the striving Right against ruthless Might,
  Wherever the bonds may bind,
Young Allen, O'Brien and Larkin die
  A ransom for all mankind.

TERESA BRAYTON

THE MARTYRED THREE
(ALLEN, LARKIN, AND O'BRIEN)

Air: The Green Above The Red

WHAT means this great and solemn throng, this dark November
  day?
With measured step, to music slow, why march along the way?
While on each gentle maiden fair and stalwart youth is seen
The mourning crape twined sadly in with Erin's emerald green.

Why now is heard, with muffled sound, the drum's dull, heavy beat?
And why swells out the mournful dirge along the city street?
Why heedless of the wintry cold and chill, downpouring rain.
March on the thousands, old and young, amidst the funeral train?

This day does weeping Erin mourn her martyred children three.
This day she bids her sons go forth, and let the tyrant see
In spite of gibbets, dungeons, chains, throughout the land are spread
Brave hearts that beat true in her cause and mourn her patriot dead.

Upon the scaffold grim they died, the last in Erin's cause.
Upon the gallows high they swung, by stern and cruel laws.
Like Emmet, Shears, Fitzgerald, Tone and hundreds true and bold,
They died to make their native land a nation as of old.

And when from bondage and from chains our country shall be free.
When o'er the land shall proudly float our flag from sea to sea,
Then shall our martyred brothers' names shine brightly side by side
Amidst the hosts who for her sake have fought and bled and died.

Now let ascend in mighty tones a nation's fervent prayer;
Let it be breathed by aged lips and by the young and fair;
On Irish tongues all o'er the world that aspiration be—
God save down-trodden Ireland and God rest her Martyred Three.

ANON

Bibliography

(*a*) GENERAL

Annual Chronicle 1867

Hansard 1867

Encyclopaedia Britannica 11th edn., Vol. 10, pp. 254–6

Two Centuries of Irish History: B.B.C. Publication 1966

Abels, J.: *The Parnell Tragedy*, The Bodley Head, London 1966

Beckett, J. C.: *The Making of Modern Ireland 1603–1923*, Faber and Faber 1965

Briggs, Asa: *Victorian People* (revised edition), Pelican Books 1965

Carty: *Ireland from the Great Famine to the Treaty of 1921*, C. J. Fallon, Dublin, 4th edn. 1966

Curtis, E.: *A History of Ireland*, Methuen, 6th edn. 1950

Davitt, M.: *The Fall of Feudalism in Ireland*, Harper & Brothers, London and New York 1904

Griffith, Arthur: *The Resurrection of Hungary*, Duffy, Gill, Sealy, Bryers & Walker, Dublin 1904

Hayes Louis, M.: *Reminiscences of Manchester from the Year 1840*, Sherratt & Hughes 1905

Jackson, T. A.: *Ireland Her Own*, Cobbett Press 1946

Le Caron: *Twenty Five Years in The Secret Service*, William Heinemann, London 1892

Leslie, Sir Shane: *The Irish Tangle*, Macdonald and Co. London 1946

Love, B.: *Handbook of Manchester*, Love & Barton, Manchester 1841

MacManus, Seamus: *The Story of the Irish Race*, The Devin Adair Company, New York 1969

Mansergh, N.: *The Irish Question*, George Allen and Unwin Ltd. 1965

O'Brien: *Parnell*, Smith and Elder and Co. 1898

O'Connor, Morris W.: *Ireland 1798–1898*, Innes and Co. Ltd. 1898

O'Hegarty, P. S.: *A History of Ireland Under The Union 1801–1922*, Methuen 1952

Joyce, P. W.: *A Concise History of Ireland*, Dublin 1917

Packenham, Thomas: *The Year of Liberty*, Hodder & Stoughton 1969

Pearse, Padraic: *Political Writings and Speeches*, Talbot Press Ltd., Dublin 1966

Sheehy Skeffington: *Life of Michael Davitt*, London 1908 and Mac-Gibbon and Kee 1967

Strauss: *Irish Nationalism and British Democracy*, Methuen 1951

(*b*) FENIAN MOVEMENT AND MANCHESTER MARTYRS

Trial and Execution of Allen and Others for Murder of Sergeant Brett, Alexander Ireland and Co., Pall Mall 1867

Bourke, Marcus: *John O'Leary*, Anvil Books Ltd., Tralee 1967

Crilly, F. L.: *The Fenian Movement, The Story of the Manchester Martyrs*, Irish Library, Vol. 2, John Ouseley Ltd. 1908

Denvir, John: *The Life Story of an Old Rebel*, Sealy, Bryers and Walker, Dublin 1910

Denvir, John: *The Irish in Britain*, Kegan, Paul and French, Trobner and Co. Ltd. 1892

Devoy, John: *Recollections*, Irish University Press 1969

Glynn, Anthony: *High Upon The Gallows Tree*, Anvill Books Ltd., Kerry 1967

Harmon: *Fenians and Fenianism*, Scepter Books, Dublin 1968. (See in particular, *The Fenians and Public Opinion in Great Britain* by Dr. Norman McCord, *The Church and the Fenians* by Donald McCortney)

Kelly, Seamus O.: *The Bold Fenian Men*, Irish News Service and Publicity, Dublin 1967

Moody, T. W.: *The Fenian Movement*, The Mercer Press, 4 Bridge Street, Cork

O'Brien and Ryan, L.: *Devoy's Postbag*, C. J. Fallon Ltd., Dublin 1948 & 1953

O'Dea: *Story of the Old Faith in Manchester*, Manchester 1910

O'Leary: *Recollections, 1896*, published more recently by the Irish University Press, with an Introduction by Marcus Bourke 1969

Rossa, J. O'Donovan: *Irish Rebels in English Prisons*, New York 1882

Rossa, J. O'Donovan: *My Years in English Jails*, Anvil Books 1967

Ryan, Desmond: *The Fenian Chief, a Biography of James Stephens*, Gill and Son, Dublin and Sydney 1967

Ryan, Desmond: *The Phoenix Flame*, Arthur Barker Ltd., London 1937

Ryan, Mark: *Fenian Memories*, M. H. Gill and Son Ltd. 1945

Smith, C. G.: *The Manchester Fenian Outrage*, Alex. Ireland & Co. 1867

Sullivan, T. D., A. M. and D. B., *Speeches From The Dock*, M. H. Gill and Co. 1945

Sullivan, T. D.: *Recollections of Troubled Times in Irish Politics*, M. H. Gill and Co. 1905

Tynan, P. J. P.: *The Irish National Invincibles and Their Times*, Chatham and Co. London 1894

(c) LABOUR HISTORY

Bright: *The Diaries of John Bright*, edited by R. A. J. Walling, Cassel & Co. Ltd., London 1930

Collins, H. and Abramsky, C.: *Karl Marx and The British Labour Movement*, Macmillan and Co. Ltd. 1965

Connolly, James: *Labour, Nationality and Religion*, Three Cables Press. *The Best of Connolly*, Mercier Press 1967

Fox Ralph: *Marx, Engels, Lenin and The Irish Revolution*, Modern Books, London

Karl Marx and Frederick Engels on Britain, Lawrence and Wishart, London 1953

Jenkins, M.: *Frederick Engels in Manchester*, Lancashire District Committee of the Communist Party

Thompson, E. P.: *The Making of the English Working Class*, Victor Gollancz and Co. 1963

(d) NEWSPAPERS AND PAMPHLETS

McGill and Redmond: *The Manchester Martyrs*, Connolly Association 1963

Manchester Martyrs Committee: *Seamus Barrett (memorial) 1857–1943*

Beehive 1867

Birmingham Daily Post 1867

Cork Examiner 1867

Daily Mail, 10th April, 1967

Dundalk Democrat 1867

Dungannon Observer, 29th April, 1967

Freeman's Journal 1867

Gaelic American 1908

Independence Belge 1867

Illustrated London News, July–Dec., 1867

Irish People

Irish Catholic Chronicle & People & News of the Week 1867

Irishman 1867–8

Irish Democrat 1967
Irish World 1908
Irish Independent 1969 ("The Fenian Tradition" by Sean Cronin)
Liberté 1867
Manchester City News 1899, 1918 and 1928
Manchester Guardian 1867
Manchester Examiner 1867
Manchester Evening Chronicle 1959 and 1960
Manchester Evening News 1935
Liverpool Mercury 1867
Nation (Dublin) 1867
New York Herald 1867
New York Times 1867
Reynolds Newspaper 1867
The Times 1867
Tipperary and Clare Independent 1867
Tipperary Vindicator 1867

Index